T0150005

THE

PTSD

SOLUTION

Also by Dr. Alan Wolfelt

Healing A Friend's Grieving Heart:
100 Practical Ideas for Helping Someone You Love Through Loss

Healing Your Grieving Heart: 100 Practical Ideas

The Journey Through Grief: Reflections on Healing

The Mourner's Book of Hope: 30 Days of Inspiration

Reframing PTSD as Traumatic Grief:
How Caregivers Can Companion Traumatized Grievers
Through Catch-Up Mourning

Understanding Your Grief:
Ten Essential Touchstones for Finding Hope
and Healing Your Heart

Companion Press is dedicated to the education and support of both the bereaved and bereavement caregivers. We believe that those who companion the bereaved by walking with them as they journey in grief have a wondrous opportunity: to help others embrace and grow through grief—and to lead fuller, more deeply-lived lives themselves because of this important ministry.

For a complete catalog and ordering information,
write, call, or visit:

Companion
PRESS

Companion Press
The Center for Loss and Life Transition
3735 Broken Bow Road
Fort Collins, CO 80526
(970) 226-6050
www.centerforloss.com

THE
PTSD
SOLUTION

The Truth about your Symptoms and How to Heal

ALAN D. WOLFELT, PH.D.

Companion
P R E S S

An imprint of the Center for Loss and Life Transition
Fort Collins, Colorado

© 2015 by Alan D. Wolfelt, Ph.D.

All rights reserved. No part of this publication may be reproduced, stored in a retrieval system, or transmitted in any form or by any means, electronic, mechanical, photocopying, recording or otherwise, without the prior permission of the publisher.

Companion Press is an imprint of the Center for Loss and Life Transition, 3735 Broken Bow Road, Fort Collins, Colorado 80526.

Printed in the United States

23 22 21 20 19 18 17 16 15   5 4 3 2 1

ISBN: 978-1-61722-226-9

To all for whom the cloud of PTSD has not yet lifted.

My hope is that this book offers you hope for your healing—
There can be light.

CONTENTS

FOREWORD

Many days I wonder if my PTSD will ever get better. Do I really want to keep going? Real sleep seems only an illusion, and the thought of falling asleep brings extreme fear and anxiety. In sleep I lose all control of which world I will enter into. Flashbacks make me feel like I am reliving the trauma. All of the sights, sounds, smells, tastes, and touch seem real.

Growing up in a military family and culture, I learned that the way you deal with the pain and suffering from trauma was to "suck it up." I was taught that emotions were for the weak. Independence and self-sufficiency—they're for the strong. Life is about winners and losers. Hardcore scientific fact and logic are the only reality. Religion and spirituality just get in the way of winning. The only moral compass you need is your gun.

Then one day love entered my life, changing my whole understanding of the world. Her name was Carolyn. She gently and patiently helped me find a new moral compass, and through the many years of our marriage, my faith and spirituality began to grow and mature. My very soul changed. I had life purpose, joy, hope, and most of all, love.

Carolyn died suddenly a few years ago from cancer. Her death marked the beginning of another life chapter, one full of depression, anxiety, fear, anger, suicidal thoughts, and sleeplessness as well as loss of friends, hope, joy, and love. My very soul felt like it had been torn apart.

Eight months after Carolyn's death, I retired after completing more than 30 years in the military. Back in 2003 Carolyn and I had started a foundation that provides financial grants to wounded vets and training for caregivers. After she died I was ready to end that mission and simply retire into my grief and pain until the end of life came.

What I did not know then was that trying to deal with Carolyn's death would only be the tip of the iceberg of my carried grief. Within me were nearly 60 years of "stuffed trauma" and the culture of war. My ability to keep all that unmourned grief in a nice, neat, secure box was about to end. All of the demons from my past were about to revisit me in a way that I had no control of. I remember telling myself I had three choices: to end my life now; live in my pain until some natural death took me; or maybe find answers to the questions of why.

I chose to ask why and began a journey of discovery. That journey led me to Dr. Alan Wolfelt.

My doctors had become concerned when my grief over Carolyn's death lasted longer than was considered acceptable. They told me I had post-traumatic stress disorder. How could I have PTSD? Through my foundation I worked with veterans every day who had PTSD, but never did I expect that I would be labeled with such a dreaded and stigmatized disability.

Dr. Wolfelt's teaching and philosophy helped me to understand what trauma is and how it injures us physically, cognitively, emotionally, socially, and spiritually. He helped me to see how traumatic grief can affect our thoughts, feelings, and behaviors.

Most of all, he helped me find a path to healing my traumatic grief. He has helped me find hope again, and with a new hope, discover a way forward to a new me. Signs of joy are returning. I am also now able to better help others dealing with traumatic grief. Life has new meaning.

The veterans I work with often ask me about the hopelessness they feel. They wonder how could I ever find hope, joy, and love again after all that I have done and gone through. I share with them—and I will share this with you—there is a way.

The healing of my traumatic grief began when my friends, family, and doctors helped me to "borrow hope" from them. When I had no hope or joy, when severe depression kept me from wanting to live, they came and shared the hope that they had in me and for me. I borrowed their hope, which has now become a new hope within me. You, too, can find a new hope. You can find a new joy. You can find a new love.

This book will guide you there. If you are feeling hopeless, then please borrow my hope for you. There is a way to find and sustain your healing as you begin to discover the truth about traumatic grief and why you are suffering. Allow the healing to start now. My thoughts and prayers are with you.

Michael Cash
Founder/CEO, Operation Family Fund

PREFACE

Understanding and helping people in grief is my life's work. As a teenager who had come to experience my own life losses, I set out to discover the principles that help people heal in grief. I earned a master's degree in psychology and then a doctorate. I completed my internship in clinical psychology at the Mayo Clinic. During these years, I also began to counsel grieving families, so that I could learn up close from grievers and those who care for them.

> "A culture that insists on seeing suffering as pathology, that is ashamed of suffering as a sign of failure or inadequacy, a culture bent on the quick fix for emotional pain, inevitably ends up denying both the social and spiritual dimensions of our sorrows."
>
> — Miriam Greenspan

Grieving people taught me a lot about authentic grief and mourning—both then and in the nearly 40 years since I've spent as a grief counselor and educator. What my formal schooling tried to teach me, on the other hand, was often less helpful. You see, according to the medical model of psychological theory, grief can be considered an illness that with proper assessment, diagnosis, and treatment can be cured. It is this same medical model, of course, that has informed and crafted our current understanding of the "disorder" or "illness" that is PTSD.

But grief is not an illness or disorder. It's what we think and feel inside when we lose something or someone we value. And since loss is a normal and unavoidable part of life, our response to loss is also normal. Loss is an injury; grief is our natural and necessary response to the injury.

Here's another way of thinking about it: Grief is love's conjoined twin. And if love is not an illness or a diagnosis, then neither is grief.

Early in my career (which I think of more as a calling), I discovered that what the medical establishment's understanding of grief really needed was a "supplement of the soul." It seemed glaringly obvious to me that as fellow travelers in the journey into grief, we needed more life-giving, hope-filled models that incorporate not only the mind and body, but more important, the soul and the spirit. I found myself resonating more with the writings of important psycho-spiritual thinkers such as Carl Jung, Viktor Frankl, James Hillman, Ram Dass, Stephen Levine, and Thomas Moore.

In fact, it was Carl Jung's writing that helped me understand that every psychological struggle is ultimately a matter of spirituality. In the end, after we as human beings mourn the many losses we encounter in life, we must find ways to (re)discover hope and meaning to go on living our tomorrows. Whether we like it or not, loss launches us on a spiritual journey of the heart and soul.

And so in my field I became a "responsible rebel"—a professional bereavement caregiver who sought to question and change the dominant professional thinking about grief. De-medicalizing grief became a central part of my life's mission. If we can see grief as the natural and necessary process that it is, and if we can also learn to encourage and support one another in the expression of our grief, we can create a culture rich in compassion and self-fulfillment. We can foster hope and healing. We can, I believe, transform the life of human beings on Earth.

In recent years, as the diagnosis of PTSD burgeoned and along with it, incidence and treatment studies as well as funding, media coverage, and general awareness, I watched and listened with interest. While I am not—and do not pretend to be—a PTSD expert (actually, I have a bit of a problem with the concept of caregiving "expertise"), I am more than an interested bystander. I am an active grief educator and thought leader who has witnessed countless times, over the course of nearly four decades, the profound harm done to grievers by a profession and culture that all too often sees grief as disease and its symptoms as pathology. We are so uncomfortable with human suffering that we characterize it as illness and want to "treat" it away.

And so, last year I took action and wrote a book for professional caregivers called *Reframing PTSD as Traumatic Grief*. In it I proposed that the medical community must start looking at PTSD through the lens of normal and necessary grief. I have been humbled by the positive response to this new resource, and I hope that as it continues to find its way into the offices of psychiatrists, psychotherapists, social workers, and other PTSD caregivers, it will spark a critical conversation about traumatic grief. With *Reframing PTSD* set on its way, I then began to work on this book, which shares the same news with the people who stand to gain the most from a revolution in thinking about PTSD: those who have suffered a traumatic event. In other words, you.

That, in a nutshell, is the path I took on the way to writing the book you hold in your hands. I believe it reveals the large and central missing piece to the puzzle of healing your PTSD. I offer it to you humbly, with compassion for your past and present and unwavering hope for your future.

Alan D. Wolfelt, Ph.D.
July 2015

INTRODUCTION

"Let today be the day you love yourself enough to no longer just dream of a better life; let it be the day you act upon it."

— Steve Maraboli

Welcome to a new way of thinking about post-traumatic stress.

If you suffer from post-traumatic stress—or what is commonly called PTSD—and continue to struggle even after trying various forms of "treatment," this book is for you. I believe that its message will help you heal.

What's more, the healing this book may help you find your way to is a deeper, fuller healing than that hoped for by most forms of PTSD treatment. The word "healing" literally means "to make whole again." In my view, the goal of post-traumatic stress treatment should not simply be to make your life tolerable again. You deserve so much more. This book starts and ends with the assumption that your life can and should be deeply meaningful, fulfilling, and joyful.

"Healing doesn't mean the damage never existed. It means the damage no longer controls our lives."

— Unknown

I am not promising nonstop happiness, of course, for life is often unhappy. In fact, the inescapability of pain in life is one of the main tenets of this book. What I am promising, however, is that this new way of thinking about post-traumatic stress and healing is a doorway to holistic well-being.

You deserve compassionate care

Another fundamental assumption in this book is that you deserve compassionate care. Something terrible happened to you or someone close to you. Something that understandably exceeded your innate capacity to cope. In essence, you suffered a serious psychic injury, and now you need and deserve excellent care.

> "Nourishing yourself in a way that helps you blossom in the direction you want to go is attainable, and you are worth the effort."
>
> — Deborah Day

Here in the twenty-first century, we all take for granted the reality that after a serious physical injury, people need intensive medical care. In fact, we have entire facilities (hospitals and clinics) and professions (doctors, nurses, and other healthcare providers) devoted to bodily care. What we need to get better at understanding and incorporating into our healthcare system is the reality that people who suffer severe psychic injuries need the same depth of comprehensive, compassionate care.

As you read this book, I also want you to keep in mind the absolute necessity of compassionate *self*-care. Just as a seriously injured accident victim is ultimately the one responsible for doing the hard work of rehabilitation—even after he leaves the direct care of hospital and rehab staff—*you* are ultimately the one responsible for your own healing. Be gentle with yourself, yes, but also never forget that you must care for yourself "with passion." That's what the word "compassion" literally means. When you do something with passion, you are actively engaged.

You are focused. You are determined. You are making it happen. You must be all of these things in your journey to healing post-traumatic stress.

You are a whole person

Yet another fundamental assumption of this book is that you are a multifaceted person. The trauma you experienced affected you physically, cognitively, emotionally, socially, and spiritually. While many medical treatments for post-traumatic stress focus on the physical and cognitive symptoms, I believe that you absolutely need and deserve holistic care. In fact, the likely reason that post-traumatic stress treatments have not fully eased your symptoms already is their lack of attention on your emotional, social, and spiritual needs.

> "What lies behind us and what lies before us are tiny matters compared to what lies within us."
> — Ralph Waldo Emerson

For human beings, our physical requirements are indeed our most fundamental needs. We literally can't survive unless we have adequate food, hydration, shelter, warmth, and safety. But once our physical needs are met, we still have other, higher-order needs—needs for social bonding, love, self-understanding, and self-fulfillment.

PTSD care that does not focus adequately—perhaps primarily—on people's emotional, social, and spiritual needs will always leave a gaping hole.

The prevalence and history of PTSD

Regardless of the source of your post-traumatic stress, regardless of your age or gender, whether your trauma was long ago or in the recent past, you are not alone. Your story is unique, but it shares many similarities with the stories of others.

Post-traumatic stress affects hundreds of millions of people worldwide. That is a staggering statistic. As our cultural and medical awareness of the condition have grown, we've begun to realize the sheer magnitude of the issue. According to the National Center for PTSD, the National Institutes of Mental Health, and the PTSD Alliance, half of all people here on Earth will experience a traumatic event at least once in their lives. About 15 percent of those people will go on to develop symptoms that meet the generally accepted medical criteria for PTSD. What's more, it's thought that women develop post-traumatic stress twice as often as men, possibly because they are more likely to be subject to interpersonal violence. The average age of post-traumatic stress onset is 23 years old.

It wasn't that long ago, however, that PTSD did not even have a name. In the twentieth century, the mental health field, like other disciplines, enjoyed an explosion of new theoretical and research-based understanding. These were the rich decades of the groundbreaking work of famous clinicians such as Sigmund Freud (in his later career), B.F. Skinner, Jean Piaget, and Carl Rogers, among other luminaries. From our early twenty-first-century vantage point, it is sometimes easy to forget that most of our understanding about mental health is less than 100 years old.

> "Just like there's always time for pain, there's always time for healing."
>
> — Jennifer Brown

While certainly human beings have experienced post-traumatic stress since the first humans walked the Earth, the term "post-traumatic stress disorder" did not appear in the guidebook clinicians use to diagnose mental health conditions, called the *Diagnostic and Statistical Manual of Mental Disorders*, or DSM for short, until the third edition was published in 1980 (after the Vietnam War). Before then, the anxiety that followed various traumatic experiences was recognized in the DSM only in piecemeal fashion, including mentions of "shell shock" and "rape trauma syndrome." Since 1980, the definition of PTSD has developed and evolved, both in professional diagnostic tools like the DSM as well as in publications and websites for the general public.

Today we live at a moment in time in which the attention and research on PTSD have exploded. PTSD is in the spotlight. The mental health professions, medical caregivers, the government, and the public all finally agree that PTSD is a legitimate problem. We're trying to figure it out. We're trying to help you and the millions of others like you.

That's the good news. The bad news is that in trying to solve the PTSD puzzle, we somehow misplaced a large and central piece. This giant hole in the middle of the puzzle has made it impossible for us to see the whole picture. It has made us incapable of adequately helping people heal their PTSD, and it has left many people with PTSD feeling frustrated, confused, angry, and hopeless. Are you one of them? Have you intuited that even if you've made some progress in healing your PTSD, something profoundly essential is still missing?

I believe I've located the missing piece, and I humbly lay it on the table in hopes that pressing it into place will reveal to all of us the solution to the puzzle of PTSD.

It's time to reconsider our thinking about post-traumatic stress

Over the centuries, humankind's understanding in every

discipline has evolved. Until better information came along, we thought that the Earth was flat, for example. Some of us believed that being photographed stole our souls. In more recent decades, we once thought that ulcers were caused by stress. Now we know they are typically caused by bacteria.

"We are all apt to believe what the world believes about us."

— George Eliot

Our understanding of post-traumatic stress is similarly evolving. In the last 20 years, modern imaging technology and lab analyses have for the first time in human history allowed us a peek inside the brain. We've begun to study the brain in more detail and actually see the areas affected by traumatic stress. We've also learned about the brain chemistry cascades and sequences triggered by frightening experiences. We've achieved a rudimentary understanding of the biochemical and brain-structural causes and effects of traumatic stress.

"Just because something has always been done in a certain way is never a sufficient reason for continuing to do it that way."

— Clarence Birdseye

These medical and scientific PTSD advancements are welcome and helpful, of course. But I believe that it's time for a second, simultaneous sea change in the thinking about PTSD. That's what this book is about.

PART ONE

WHAT IF?

This book and the thinking it contains about post-traumatic stress are probably different than what you've heard before. The reason they're different has to do with my belief in asking "'What if?"

Here are the main "What if?" questions that form the foundation of this book. Please join me in asking and attempting to answer them.

> "If there is something to gain and nothing to lose by asking, by all means, ask."
>
> — W. Clement Stone

What if you do not have an illness or disorder but instead an injury?

Post-traumatic stress is commonly diagnosed as an illness, disease, or disorder. Let's think about those terms for a moment. An illness or disease is an intrinsic, internal going-awry. It is a malfunction within us. The word "disorder" describes a similar internal flaw or impairment but is often applied to mental, or brain, health.

> "I want to show that the dividing lines between sanity and mental illness have been drawn in the wrong place."
>
> — Anthony Storr

An injury, on the other hand, is the result of an external blow. When we are injured, something physically and often violently happens to us. Injury is the effect of an outside action.

When we experience a traumatic event, something significant and often sudden, violent, and horrible outside our control happens *to* us. When it happens, we sustain an injury. We might be bodily injured, of course, but even when we are not, our psyches are injured in a way that creates often severe physical, cognitive, emotional, social, and spiritual symptoms.

Traumatic events injure us. They do not make us sick or ill.

But wait. Why does the distinction between illness and injury I am trying to make matter in the first place? The chief reason is that the terms "illness," "disease," and "disorder" carry a stigma. When someone has heart disease or cancer, for example, we tend to place, consciously or unconsciously, a degree of blame on the sick person. After all, he might have done something that contributed to or made him more susceptible to the illness. While this rationale is occasionally true, it's often untrue. And so, while our tendency to stigmatize illness is also unfortunate and also needs to change, let's call traumatic stress what it is—an injury—as part of our effort to de-stigmatize it.

Mental health illnesses, in particular, suffer from stigmatization. We tend to blame people for their own mental illnesses, as if they somehow should be more capable of controlling them than illnesses

TRAUMATIC BRAIN INJURY

Many military veterans as well as people who have experienced violent accidents and natural disasters have PTSD and traumatic brain injuries (TBI). In other words, in addition to a psychic injury to the brain, heart, and soul, this subset of people with PTSD has also suffered a physical injury to the brain, which compounds common PTSD symptoms and also creates additional symptoms. If you have a TBI in addition to post-traumatic stress, you need and deserve well-coordinated care among medical and mental health caregivers. You will need extra care and compassion, including self-compassion.

that occur from the neck down. Again, this thinking is antiquated and harmful and, thank goodness, oh-so-slowly changing. But in the meantime, because PTSD falls into the mental health category and is in the DSM, under the oversight of psychiatrists instead of general physicians, when we think of PTSD as an illness, its stigma is multiplied. What if we instead were to think of it as a sort of brain injury? Doesn't that immediately make it a more sympathetic condition, one deserving of everyone's compassion and patience? I believe it does.

What's more, the terms "disorder," "disease," and "illness" can seem more permanent than "injury." Many diseases are incurable or chronic, right? Disorders are often forever. The concept of injury, on the other hand, implies that the symptoms are something that, with appropriate attention, can and will heal. The idea of injury is essentially more hopeful.

> "The struggle you're in today is developing the strength you need for tomorrow. Don't give up."
>
> — Robert Tew

You may be one of the millions of people worldwide to have been formally diagnosed with PTSD. If you were, you were probably told you have an illness or disorder. This categorization and the stigma that comes with it may well have made you feel a sense of shame. If so, I would like you to take off the cloak of shame and throw it away. You are not sick; you were injured. It is not your fault. You did nothing wrong. Now try on the injury understanding instead. You were and are injured. How does it make you feel to know that you are injured instead of ill?

I count myself among the people now calling for the "D" to be dropped from PTSD. It is not a disorder. It is a normal and natural response to a serious injury. While I will occasionally use the acronym PTSD in the remainder of this book, I do so only because we are all familiar with it and because at times it works as the best, most expedient shorthand.

What if your symptoms are normal and necessary responses to this injury?

When you are injured physically, your body's response to the injury depends on the severity of the injury.

If you accidentally bump into a wall, you might say "Ow!" and later notice a small bruise, but that will be the extent of it. Yet if you are badly injured in a car accident, you may be rushed to the emergency room by an ambulance, undergo surgery, and spend weeks recuperating in the hospital, followed by months of physical therapy, pain management, and other treatments.

> "We're getting rid of the D. PTS is an injury; it's not a disorder. The problem is when you call it a disorder, [people] don't think they can be treated."
>
> — George W. Bush

The same pattern holds true for psychic injuries. Your response to the injury will depend on its severity.

We suffer psychic injuries all the time, but most of them are relatively mild. Remember, we have said that injuries are caused by external factors. An example of a mild psychic injury might be an unkind remark by a friend or family member. Another might be the sudden (but not life-threatening) illness of a child or news of a dear neighbor's impending move to another part of town.

All of these things may "hurt" us, if only for a moment or a day or two. We feel a twinge of sadness, panic, concern, fear, regret, despair, and/or other painful emotions. And then typically we incorporate these everyday injuries into our understanding of how life works and we move forward.

But sometimes we experience more profound psychic injuries. A spouse says she no longer loves us and wants a divorce. We are fired from a job we like or need—a job that may also form the lion's share of our identity. A child estranges himself from us. A loved one dies. The particulars of how we feel inside and how we behave outside after these kinds of blows depend on many factors, but it is safe to say that the more profound the psychic injury, the more extreme our pain, our thoughts, our feelings, and our behaviors.

You suffered a severe psychic injury of a particular kind—one that was likely sudden and violent. And if you believe or have been told that you are suffering from post-traumatic stress, that means your physical, cognitive, emotional, social, and spiritual responses to this injury have been relatively extreme. Your symptoms may have been serious enough that they prevented you from completing essential daily activities and interacting lovingly with others.

A mild injury causes minor symptoms, while an extreme injury causes severe symptoms. This may seem like a ridiculously obvious claim, but it's one that doesn't seem to be fully respected by the current thinking about post-traumatic stress.

The severe symptoms of post-traumatic stress are, I believe, normal and necessary. That is, when they exist, that means they are normal and necessary for the person who experiences them. While they may be painful and frightening, they are not bad. They are not wrong. They simply are. Just as leg pain or internal bleeding or heart-rhythm problems are not "wrong" after a serious car accident, severe post-traumatic stress symptoms are not "wrong" after a severe traumatic experience.

Do you see how your post-traumatic stress can be understood as an extreme reaction caused by an extreme external reality?

Whatever it consists of, your post-traumatic stress is your unique but natural response to a serious injury. We'll talk more later about why your post-traumatic stress might seem more or less severe than that of someone else who experienced a similar trauma, but for now I hope you'll agree to think of your symptoms as a normal and necessary response to the psychic injury you suffered.

"Sanity remains defined simply by the ability to cope with insane conditions."

— Ana Castillo

You are not abnormal. There is nothing inherently "wrong" with you. You are not ill, sick, or diseased. Instead, you are profoundly injured, and you deserve equally profound understanding and care.

What if post-traumatic stress is really a form of grief?

When we hear the word "grief," we tend to think of death. Grief is what we feel after someone we love dies, right? This is true. But this understanding of grief is also far too narrow. Actually, grief is what we think and feel whenever something we value is harmed or taken away.

"Pain is the difference between what is and what I want it to be."

— Spencer Johnson

And so, we grieve after divorce. We grieve when we are diagnosed with cancer. We grieve when our children grow up and move away. We grieve all the time, because life is full of bittersweet transitions and painful losses.

When we experience a traumatic event, we also suffer losses.

What those losses are depends on the circumstances of the event. We may lose someone we care about. We may lose some aspect of our health. We may lose our home or belongings. We may lose our trust in others. We often lose our sense of safety and predictability in the world around us. We often lose, for a time, our ability to think clearly. This is to name just a few of the many, many losses that may affect you (consciously or subconsciously) in the aftermath of a traumatic event.

THINGS WE GRIEVE OVER AFTER A TRAUMATIC EVENT

PRIMARY AND SECONDARY LOSSES

All significant losses create a ripple effect of other losses. When someone I love dies, for example, I lose much more than the physical presence of that person (the primary loss). Depending on the roles that person played in my life, I may also feel that I have lost my history (if the person was a parent or sibling), my financial security (if the person was a financial provider), and/or my sense of immortality (any death).

The traumatic event you experienced may or may not have caused what we think of as a primary loss. During a tornado, for instance, I may lose my house or belongings. Or someone I care about might be injured or even killed. Those would be considered primary losses. But even if those things don't happen to me, if the tornado came near to me or to people I care about, I will still be affected by secondary losses.

Here's a partial list of what I mean by "secondary losses."

LOSS OF SENSE OF SECURITY

- Physical security: Because of the body's fight-or-flight response, people who experience a traumatic event commonly feel physically unsafe.

- Emotional security: Emotions may feel out-of-control. Friends and family who had always provided emotional support may now step away.

- Financial security: The event might have caused costly damage.

Also, post-traumatic stress sufferers whose symptoms prevent them from working may end up with serious money problems.

LOSS OF SELF
- Self: "I feel like part of me got left behind at the traumatic event."
- Identity: Post-traumatic stress sufferers sometimes have to rethink their roles as employees, husbands or wives, mothers or fathers, sons or daughters, best friends, etc.
- Self-confidence: People with post-traumatic stress commonly experience negative self-esteem.
- Health: The physical symptoms of of fight-or-flight or freeze as well as normal grief can create a feeling of physical unwellness.
- Personality: "I just don't feel like myself."

LOSS OF MEANING
- Goals and dreams: Hopes and dreams for the future can be shattered.
- Faith: People who've experienced a traumatic event often question their faith.
- Will/desire to live: People with post-traumatic stress may question their futures. They may ask, "Why go on?"
- Joy: Life's most precious emotion, happiness, is naturally compromised after a traumatic event.

As with all loss, the many losses caused by a traumatic event naturally give rise to grief. We cannot help but grieve after loss. We cannot help but grieve after a traumatic event causes losses in our lives. We automatically grieve. Everything we think and feel inside about the event or as a result of the event, in fact, *is* our grief. In this book I will talk a lot about grief, and it is this broader understanding of the word "grief" that I ask you to bring to bear on this chapter and all those that follow.

Grief isn't just sadness, by the way. It can also be feelings of shock, denial, disorganization, confusion, anger, fear, and panic. It may be regret and sometimes relief. It's physical pain and social discomfort. It is often disjointed thinking and spiritual despair. It's all of that, mixed up into a soup whose specific ingredients and intensity of flavor change from day to day, week to week, month to month.

Does that soup sound at all like your post-traumatic stress? If so, we might be onto something here.

PART TWO:

THE GRIEF WE CALL PTSD

If you've been diagnosed with PTSD or care about someone who has, you probably have a solid understanding of what is meant by the term. But to review, the website of the National Center for PTSD, which is a division of the U.S. Department of Veterans Affairs (the VA), defines PTSD in this way:

"PTSD isn't about what's wrong with you. It's about what happened to you."

— Unknown

After a trauma or life-threatening event, it is common to have reactions such as upsetting memories of the event, increased jumpiness, or trouble sleeping. If these reactions do not go away or if they get worse, you may have Posttraumatic Stress Disorder (PTSD).

In its turn, the website of the National Institute of Mental Health (NIMH) offers this explanation of PTSD:

When in danger, it's natural to feel afraid. This fear triggers many split-second changes in the body to prepare to defend against the danger or to avoid it. This 'fight or flight' response is a healthy reaction meant to protect a person from harm. But in post-traumatic stress disorder (PTSD), this reaction is changed or damaged. People who have PTSD may feel stresses or frightened even when they're no longer in danger.

PTSD develops after a terrifying ordeal that involved physical harm or the threat of physical harm. The person who develops PTSD may have been the one who was harmed, the harm may have happened to a loved one, or the person may have witnessed a harmful event that happened to loved ones or strangers.

PTSD happens because horrible things happen to people. PTSD was first brought to public attention in relation to war veterans, but it can result from a variety of traumatic incidents, including (but not limited to) mugging, rape, torture, being kidnapped or held captive, child abuse, car accidents, train wrecks, plane crashes, bombings, or natural disasters such as fires, floods, and earthquakes. (Note that most of these experiences are single events, often short in duration, occurring one time. That is why I will use the term "traumatic event" throughout this book. However, some traumatic experiences, such as sexual abuse or military combat, often occur over a longer period of time and are not single "events." They are really better described as "ongoing traumatic experiences." But for simplicity's sake, when I say "traumatic event," I mean to include both categories.)

MORAL INJURY AND PTSD

In your quest to understand and heal from your post-traumatic stress symptoms, you may have encountered the term "moral injury." Often associated with combat veterans, moral injury is a psychic injury caused by the violation of one's own core moral beliefs. War often forces service members to carry out or participate in actions that deep down they believe are morally wrong, though war is not the only possible arena for moral injury.

Regardless of the how or the why, when people go against their own conscience, even if it seemed the right or only thing to do at the time, they often sustain a deep psychic injury. In the aftermath they typically feel overwhelming guilt, worthlessness, remorse, and despair. They may be depressed and turn to addictive substances or activities for relief. Depending on the source of the moral injury, they may or may not also have the terrible fear-based symptoms associated with PTSD.

I believe that moral injury is also a form of a grief because what violating one's own core beliefs does is create losses. Loss of innocence. Loss of self-esteem. Loss of trust in self and others. It is these and the other very significant losses caused by the morally repugnant event or ongoing situation that gives rise to feelings of guilt, remorse, despair, etcetera.

There is only one way to come to terms with the many painful thoughts and feelings associated with loss, and that is to mourn— or express—them. We'll talk a lot more about mourning later in this book, but for now, please know that if you believe you have sustained a moral injury, you are in the right place. Welcome.

Diagnostic criteria for PTSD

Now let's look a little more closely at the diagnostic criteria for PTSD. As we've said, mental health clinicians use a book called *The Diagnostic and Statistical Manual*, or DSM, which is created and published by the American Psychiatric Association, to diagnose mental health problems. It's their 991-page Bible. The most recent edition, the DSM-5, published in 2013, contains detailed descriptions of about 300 mental health conditions as well as defining onset, symptoms, duration, and other criteria for each.

If you were diagnosed with PTSD, you were probably diagnosed by a healthcare provider who relies on (or at least has a working understanding of) the DSM.

According to the DSM, the primary PTSD symptoms involve the

re-experiencing or repeated intrusion of the event, including

a) thoughts or perception,

b) images,

c) dreams,

d) illusions or hallucinations,

e) dissociative flashbacks, and/or

f) psychological and physiological reactions to cues that remind the person of the event.

The DSM-5 says that at least one of these things must be persistently occurring.

The remaining symptoms involve **avoidance**, **negative cognition and mood**, and **hyper-arousal**.

Avoidance is essential to the diagnosis. People who avoid thoughts, feelings, or conversations about the event OR activities, places, or other people that remind them of the event are considered to be exhibiting avoidance. The DSM-5 says one of these must be present.

Negative alteration in cognition and mood can include an inability to remember significant aspects of the event; persistent and exaggerated negative beliefs about oneself, others, and the world; persistent, distorted thoughts about the cause or consequences of the event; persistent negativity; markedly diminished interest or participation in significant activities; feelings of detachment or estrangement from others; and/or a persistent inability to experience positive emotions. The DSM-5 says two or more of these symptoms must be present.

Hyper-arousal symptoms are those we think of as being connected to fear and fight-or-flight: difficulty sleeping; irritability or aggressive behavior; self-destructive or reckless behavior; difficulty concentrating; hyper-vigilance; and exaggerated startle response. At least two of these must be present, according to the DSM-5.

Finally, to meet the DSM-5 definition of PTSD, the symptoms must have been **present for at least a month** and must also be **causing significant distress or functional impairment**.

Now that we're clear on the by-the-book medical criteria for PTSD, let's take a look at the common symptoms of everyday, garden-variety—or what therapists often call "uncomplicated"—grief.

> "The best way out is always through."
>
> — Robert Frost

What is grief?

Grief is a mixture of ever-changing thoughts and feelings that stem from loss. It's that soup I mentioned at the end of Part One.

Below are the most common symptoms of typical, uncomplicated grief. Again, keep in mind that these symptoms usually occur after any significant loss—not just the death of someone loved.

Shock, numbness, denial, and disbelief

"It feels like a dream," people in early grief often say. "I feel like I might wake up and none of this will have happened." They also say, "I was there, but yet I really wasn't. I managed to do what needed to be done, but I didn't feel a part of it."

Shock, numbness, and disbelief are nature's way of temporarily protecting grievers from the full reality of a loss. Much as physical shock shuts down unnecessary bodily functions (such as digestion) to ensure the heart keeps beating and the lungs keep breathing, emotional shock helps insulate people psychologically until they are more able to tolerate what they aren't ready to believe.

This mixture of shock, numbness, and disbelief acts as an anesthetic: the pain exists, but grievers may not experience it fully. Typically, a physical component also accompanies feelings of shock. The autonomic nervous system is affected and may cause heart palpitations, queasiness, stomach pain, dizziness, and other bodily symptoms.

Disorganization, confusion, searching, and yearning
Maybe the most isolating and frightening part of early grief is the sense of disorganization, confusion, searching, and yearning that often follows the loss. These feelings frequently arise when the griever begins to be confronted with the reality of the loss.

People express disorganization and confusion in their inability to complete tasks. They may start to do something but never finish. They may feel forgetful and ineffective, especially early in the morning and late at night, when fatigue and lethargy are most prominent.

When someone loved has died, they may experience a restless searching for the person. Yearning and preoccupation with memories can leave grievers feeling drained. They can even experience a shift in perception: other people may begin to look like the person who died.

Other common, related experiences include difficulties eating and sleeping. Grievers may experience a loss of appetite or find themselves overeating. Even when they do eat, they may be unable to taste the food. Having trouble falling asleep and early morning awakening are also common experiences associated with this dimension of grief.

Anxiety, panic, and fear

Feelings of anxiety, panic, and fear are common components of the grief experience. Grievers ask themselves, "Am I going to be OK? Will I survive this?" These questions are natural. The grievers' sense of security has been threatened, so they are naturally anxious.

A variety of thoughts and situations can increase anxiety, panic, and fear. For example, grievers may be afraid of what the future holds or that they will experience other losses. They may be more aware of their own vulnerability or mortality, which can be scary. They may feel panicky about their inability to concentrate. Financial problems can compound feelings of anxiety.

Anxiety and depression often go hand-in-hand. In fact, surveys show that 60 to 70 percent of people with depression also have anxiety, and half of people with anxiety also have significant depression. They are now thought by many mental health caregivers to be two faces of one symptom.

Explosive emotions

Anger, hate, blame, terror, resentment, rage, and jealousy are explosive, volatile, yet natural parts of the grief journey. It helps to understand that all these feelings are, at bottom, a form of protest. Think of the toddler whose favorite toy is yanked out of his hands. This toddler wants the toy: when it's taken, his instinctive reaction may be to scream or cry or hit. When someone or something you care about is taken from you, your instinctive reaction may be much the same.

> "A wise therapist taught me that anger is the emotion we snatch up to avoid less comfortable feelings—confusion, fear, sadness."
>
> — Jill Herzig

Explosive emotions can surface at any time during the grief journey. Grievers may direct these emotions at a person who died or left (such as in divorce), at the organization that caused the loss (such as a job lay-off), at friends and family members, at doctors, at people who haven't experienced loss, at God. People sometimes oversimplify explosive emotions by looking only at anger, but grievers may experience a whole range of intense feelings such as those listed above. Underneath these emotions are usually feelings of pain, helplessness, fear, hurt, and frustration.

Guilt and regret

Guilt, regret, and self-blame are common and natural feelings after a loss. Grievers often have a case of the "if-onlys":

If only I had gotten him to the doctor sooner...

If only I had been more... If only I hadn't...

Other potential aspects of guilt and regret include the following:

- *Survivor guilt* - Sometimes being alive, unharmed, or directly unaffected when someone they care about has died, been injured, or directly affected by a harmful event can foster survivor guilt in grievers.

- *Relief-guilt* - Grievers sometimes feel relieved if they have been spared the worst effects of a loss event. But feelings of relief can also make them feel guilty. "I shouldn't be feeling relieved," they may think.

- *Joy-guilt* - Like relief-guilt, joy-guilt is about thinking that happy feelings are bad at a time of loss. One day grievers might find themselves smiling or laughing at something, only to chastise themselves for having felt happy for a minute.

Sadness and depression

Grievers often describe sadness as the most painful feeling on the journey through grief. Even in normal, uncomplicated grief, it often takes weeks or months after the loss event before grievers arrive at the full depth of their sorrow. Relatedly, depression and its accompanying anhedonia—which means, literally, a state of being "without pleasure"—are also extremely common in grief.

Relief

In normal grief, feelings of relief and release are common, especially when the loss includes some element of "it's finally over." If you are laid off or fired from a job that you needed for the paycheck but hated, you will probably feel relief as well as other symptoms of grief. If someone dies who in life abused you, you may well feel a sense of relief. The expression of normal grief thoughts and feelings also commonly causes feelings of relief and release. "I feel so much better now that I've said that," people often say to me.

In grief, all of these symptoms can be mild, extreme, or somewhere in between. Their severity often depends on the degree of attachment the person who is grieving felt to the person or thing that was lost as well as a number of other factors. For example, if I am deeply in love with my wife but learn, seemingly out of the blue, that she wants a divorce, my grief will probably feel severe. I am likely to experience deeper shock, anxiety, anger, and sadness than someone who feels less attached to his wife or marriage. The other factors that will influence my unique grief will include my personal loss history, my personality, my age and gender, my religious and cultural background, and more.

What's more, the individual symptoms of grief tend to overlap one another as well as wax and wane independently. I might feel angry one week but not the next. I might feel deeply sad for a while, less sad for a time, then really sad again.

You might have heard of the "stages of grief," popularized in 1969 by Elisabeth Kübler-Ross's landmark text, *On Death and Dying*. In this book she lists the five stages of grief that she saw terminally ill patients experience in the face of their own impending deaths: denial, anger, bargaining, depression, and acceptance. However, she never intended for her five stages to be applied to all grief or to be interpreted as a rigid, linear sequence to be followed by all mourners. As I've said, grief is more like a soup than a step-by-step process.

The fear factor

You know that fear-based symptoms are prominent in PTSD, but what you may not realize is that they're also very common in grief. So let's zoom in on them in order to compare them side-by-side.

Fear in traumatic grief

Traumatic events create a unique, two-part grief experience: one focused on the event itself and one focused on the primary and secondary losses the event caused. The part focused on the event itself is the source of the fear-based symptoms, such as anxiety and flashbacks, that are typically so dominant in PTSD.

We have evolutionary biology to thank for the fear-based symptoms of post-traumatic stress. When we are under imminent threat, our ancient fight-or-flight system kicks in. This is the biological wiring that evolved to keep us alive in dangerous situations.

If I suddenly notice that a predator—a grizzly bear, say—is nearby and is approaching me, my brain recognizes "Danger!"

and activates my sympathetic nervous system and my adrenal-corticol system, setting a cascade of physical responses in motion. My sympathetic nervous system uses nerve pathways in my body to initiate reactions, while my adrenal-corticol system releases hormones through the bloodstream.

My brain's amygdalae, two small clusters of cells deep in my temporal lobes that are in charge of emotional processing, interpret what I am seeing as danger and instantly send a distress signal to my hypothalamus. My hypothalamus is my stress command center, in charge of my autonomic nervous system. It reaches out to my adrenal glands, which pump out epinephrine, a.k.a. adrenaline.

My heart rate increases, pushing blood to my muscles, heart, and other vital organs.

My breathing rate increases so I can take in more oxygen.

My digestion slows down or stops, because it's not necessary right now.

My blood vessels constrict to channel blood to my muscles.

My pupils dilate so I can see better.

My brain receives the extra oxygen and goes into hyper-alert status.

In short, my body prepares to either run away or stay and fight.

After the initial surge of adrenaline subsides, if I am still seeing that scary grizzly bear (instead of realizing at this point that what I saw was just a bear-shaped shadow), my hypothalamus activates what is known as the HPA (hypothalamic-pituitary-adrenal) axis. This second punch in the one-two punch stress response *keeps* my body in hyper-alert mode. My pituitary releases a hormone called *adrenocorticotropic hormone*, or ACTH, which travels to my adrenal glands, prompting them to release cortisol. Also called "the stress hormone," cortisol maintains my body's fluid balance and blood pressure and checks non-essential bodily functions, such as reproductive drive, immunity, and growth.

All of this (and more) happens without my conscious awareness or permission.

Instead, my body's reaction to danger is subconscious and primal. The name that we use to describe what my body is feeling is "fear." I see danger, so I feel fear. In other words, fear is what it feels like in my body when my body's primal fight-or-flight system has been activated.

For millennia, fear has kept us alive. When we are in true physical danger, it still does. You'd better believe that if I encounter a grizzly bear on my next hike in the northern Rocky Mountains, I'll be grateful for fear. But now that human societies and technologies have evolved to the point that in our daily lives we rarely experience imminent life-or-death situations, our fear response is more likely to take up residence as chronic worry and anxiety.

As you may know, the new science of PTSD has determined that the fight-or-flight system that activates when we experience a traumatic event can essentially become stuck. If I survive a close call with a tornado, for example, it is my fight-or-flight system that may have propelled me to the basement. As the tornado passed overhead and I experienced the terror of the sounds and sensations of horrific winds, flying debris,

"After a traumatic experience, the human system of self-preservation seems to go onto permanent alert, as if the danger might return at any moment."

— Judith Lewis Herman

and collapsing structures—as well as, possibly, injury to myself or the injury or death of others—naturally I continue to feel fear and remain in fight-or-flight or sometimes freeze mode.

But after the tornado is long gone, in the weeks and months after the experience, if I still feel numb and anxious and can't seem to shake the intrusive, horrific memories of what it was like to live through the horror of this natural disaster, I may be diagnosed with PTSD.

Developments in technology in the last 20 or so years, especially functional MRIs, have allowed researchers to image the brains of people affected by PTSD. One finding has been that people with PTSD have much more spontaneous brain activity in their amygdalae. In other words, even when they are in a totally safe and quiet environment, people with PTSD have amygdalae that are still "firing." In addition, even in people whose PTSD symptoms have eased, the amygdalae have been found to be smaller in size.

Another lingering brain effect of PTSD seems to reside in the brain's hippocampi, which lie next to the amygdalae and are the center of memory storage and recall. While the amygdala detects threats, the hippocampus links the fear response to the context—the place, the time, the people—in which the threat is happening. Some studies indicate that, like the amygdala, the hippocampus shrinks after a traumatic event, possibly due to an overdose of cortisol. It is thought that the damaged hippocampi may prevent flashbacks and nightmares from being properly processed and/or may cause difficulty recalling parts of the traumatic event. You might think of the injured hippocampus as a glitchy hard drive.

It is also thought that the HPA axis may become chronically disrupted in PTSD. Studies of children who lost a parent in the September 11, 2001, terrorist attacks, for example, showed persistent HPA axis dysregulation in the form of continuously elevated cortisol levels two years after the event.

PTSD is also sometimes referred to as a disease of memory. In an article by J. Douglas Bremmer, M.D., of Yale University School of Medicine and the National Center for PTSD, the author explains that victims of childhood abuse often have troubles with declarative memory (remembering facts) and atypical gaps in memory that span minutes or days.

After studying the brains of childhood abuse victims and comparing them to the brains of Vietnam combat veterans, he and his team concluded that trauma causes measurable physical changes to the brain's hippocampi as well as the medial prefrontal cortex, which is the part of the brain tasked with planning and decision-making. These changes, the researchers believe, are what lead not only to classic PTSD symptoms (such as the psychological fear response to cues that remind the person of the trauma event and selective amnesia of the trauma event) but also to future, seemingly unrelated memory problems (such as difficulty learning and remembering new information).

Still, here in the first quarter of the twenty-first century, the brain is still largely a mystery, and researchers are just beginning to identify and understand the biological basis of PTSD. It is truly wonderful that medical science continues to create ever-clearer instruction manuals to the biology of the human body. The brain seems to be the last great frontier of medical science, and its study has already led to astonishing improvements in the treatment of diseases like clinical depression, Parkinson's, and paralysis. Some researchers and thinkers believe that one day soon we will be able to yoke the biology of the brain and technology together to do things like record memories and play them in someone else's head and re-upload memories into the brains of people with Alzheimer's. All I can say is *Wow!*

So yes, brain research is fascinating and can certainly yield practical, useful results. You yourself may appreciate understanding the biochemistry behind your fear-based PTSD symptoms. You may even have been helped by therapies that are based on this biochemical understanding. Yet where the medical establishment considers brain research in PTSD the Holy Grail, I believe it can only ever solve part of the puzzle. I part ways with the strictly biochemical approach to PTSD and the technologies that can interact with that biochemistry because of my belief in the soul.

Do you think we are nothing more than the composite of our molecules, cells, and synapses? If so, then the medical approach to PTSD may be all you require.

If, on the other hand, you believe, as I do, that the consciousness of human beings exists *apart from* our bodies and may pre-exist and continue on in some form after the death of our bodies, then a physical-only model of PTSD assessment and treatment is sorely lacking. The brain's architecture and the biochemical markers of PTSD are just part of the picture.

> "Spirituality is the science of the soul."
>
> — Swami Vivekananda

Here's another key question: Do you believe love is a condition that cannot be fully grasped as a mere biochemical reaction? Do you believe in the intrinsically spiritual nature of life and death? Do you believe that loss creates grief, which is foremost and fundamentally a spiritual journey—not a biochemical disorder—

of the heart and soul? If your answer to these three questions is "Maybe" or "Yes," I invite you to read on.

Fear in uncomplicated grief
It's also essential to understand that traumatic grief does not have an exclusive claim on fear-based symptoms. The body's fight-or-flight response is activated with loss of any kind. Consider how you feel when, say, you are out shopping and realize your wallet is missing.

> "No one ever told me that grief felt so like fear."
>
> — C.S. Lewis

Your heart rate increases, pushing blood to your muscles, heart, and other vital organs.

Your breathing rate increases so you can take in more oxygen.

Your pupils dilate so you can see better.

Your brain receives the extra oxygen and goes into hyper-alert status.

In other words, your body tenses for action, and so you feel a sudden jolt of fear.

The same thing happens when you first learn of significant losses in your life, like the loss of a job, a request for separation or divorce from a partner, and, of course, the death of a loved one.

In cases in which the fear response to a loss isn't merely a temporary warning—"Oh, no! Where's my wallet? Oh, now I remember! I put it in my jacket pocket. Here it is!"— phase two of the fight-or-flight response also kicks in. The HPA axis is activated, leading to the release of the stress hormone cortisol to *keep* you in hyper-alert mode.

As with PTSD, however, the lingering fight-or-flight response in the face of profound loss can be a challenge. After all, we cannot run away from our losses. And we typically can't fight them either. While our fear response might help us find our wallet, try to get our job back (or find another job), and search for ways to put our marriage back on track, it cannot magically reverse most losses. Whether we fight the change or not, jobs sometimes disappear. Marriages dissolve. And people we love die.

So when we are grieving, we are often left with this feeling of fear, which transforms over time into worry and anxiety. In grief, anxiety is typically generated from thoughts such as: "Will my life have any purpose after this loss? Will I ever be happy again? I don't think I can live like this." We also worry that in the wake of one loss, we are vulnerable to more losses. "What if my wife loses her job, too? What if my children won't want to spend time with me after the divorce? What if other people I love die?" Significant loss naturally threatens our feelings of security and stability, and so it is normal to worry and feel anxious.

> "The world is indeed full of peril, and in it there are many dark places; but still there is much that is fair, and though in all lands love is now mingled with grief, it grows perhaps the greater."
> — J.R.R. Tolkien

When we lose something or someone we value, it's also common for us to feel like we're "going crazy," which in turn compounds our fear. Because normal thoughts and behaviors in grief are so different from what one normally experiences, the grieving person does not know whether her new thoughts and behaviors are normal or abnormal.

The person who is grieving often feels a sense of restlessness, agitation, impatience, and ongoing confusion. An analogy that seems to fit is that grief is like being in the middle of a wild, rushing river, where you can't get a grasp on anything. Disconnected thoughts race through the griever's mind, and strong emotions at times are overwhelming. Disorganization and confusion often express themselves as an inability to complete any task. Projects may get started but go unfinished. Time is distorted and seen as something to be endured. Often, early morning and late at night are moments when the griever feels most disoriented and confused.

Disorganization and confusion are often accompanied by fatigue and lack of initiative, what I often call "the lethargy of grief." The acute pain of the loss is devastating to the point that normal pleasures do not seem to matter. Anhedonia, which is a technical term meaning "the inability to experience pleasure," and listlessness set in.

If the loss was the death of a loved one, a restless searching for the person who died is a common part of the experience. Yearning for the dead person and being preoccupied with memories of him may lead to intense moments of distress. Often a shift in perception makes the griever think that other people look like the dead person. A phenomenon sometimes exists whereby sounds are interpreted as signals that the person has returned, such as hearing the garage door open and the person entering the house as she had done for so many years. In fact, visual hallucinations occur so frequently in normal grief that they cannot be considered abnormal. I personally prefer the term "memory picture" to visual hallucination. Seemingly, as part of the searching and yearning process, the griever not only experiences a sense of the dead person's presence but may have transient experiences of looking across the room and seeing the person.

Dreams about the loss are also often a part of the normal grief experience. In the case of the death of someone loved, dreams are often an unconscious means of searching for the person who died. These dreams are often described to me by people as an opportunity to be close to the person. As one widower related, "I don't seem to have any control over it, but each night I find myself dreaming about my wife. I see us together, happy and content. If it only could be that way again." For other people, the dreams are not happy but rather nightmares in which they re-experience the loss or strive to overturn the loss, only to be thwarted.

And so, ongoing fear, worry, and anxiety can be as much a part of normal grief as they are a part of PTSD. Likewise, disorganization, confusion, flashbacks, hallucinations/memory pictures, and nightmares are also common in uncomplicated grief.

PTSD versus grief

Now that we've reviewed the DSM-required symptoms for a PTSD diagnosis as well as the most common symptoms of normal, uncomplicated grief that I have witnessed or that have been described to me in my nearly four decades as a grief counselor and educator, and we've also zoomed in on the fear-based symptoms of both, it's time to compare PTSD and grief. Let's look at them side-by-side in this chart:

SYMPTOM	PTSD	NORMAL GRIEF
Thoughts or perception about the event/loss	✔	✔
Images of the event/loss	✔	✔
Dreams about the event/loss	✔	✔
Illusions or hallucinations	✔	✔

(continued on next page)

SYMPTOM	PTSD	NORMAL GRIEF
Dissociative flashbacks	✔	Sometimes
Psychological or physical reactions to cues	✔	✔
An inability to remember significant aspects of the event	✔	Sometimes
Avoiding thoughts, feelings, conversations, places, or people that are reminders	✔	✔
Persistent and negative beliefs about self, others, or world	✔	Sometimes
Persistent, distorted thoughts about the cause or consequences of the event/loss	✔	Sometimes
Persistent negativity	✔	Sometimes
Markedly diminished interest or participation in significant activities	✔	✔
Feelings of detachment or estrangement from others; self-isolating behavior	✔	✔
Persistent inability to experience positive emotions; anhedonia	✔	✔
Difficulty sleeping	✔	✔
Irritability or anger outbursts; explosive emotions	✔	✔
Difficulty concentrating; disorganization, confusion	✔	✔
Hyper-vigilance	✔	Sometimes
Exaggerated startle response; anxiety, panic, fear	✔	✔

Though this comparison doesn't try to capture the subtle differences between typical PTSD symptoms and uncomplicated grief, such as *degree* or *duration* of irritability or hallucinations, for example, it does, at a glance, tell us that the two injury responses have a lot in common.

If we were to illustrate this as a Venn diagram, it might look something like this:

Basically, the fear-based symptoms are often more prominent in PTSD, but otherwise, PTSD and grief can and sometimes do look, sound, and feel almost exactly alike.

That's no coincidence. That's because PTSD is a kind of grief.

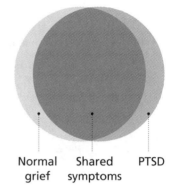

Normal grief   Shared symptoms   PTSD

Traumatic grief

PTSD is a kind of grief I'm going to call "traumatic grief."

More specifically, PTSD is grief that is set in motion by a traumatic event. While the DSM says that only certain types of what it calls "inciting events" or "stressors" count toward a diagnosis of PTSD, you and I can be more flexible. Let's say that a "trauma" is any event (or ongoing experience) of such intensity, brutality, or magnitude of horror that it would overwhelm the capacity to cope for many of us.

> "PTSD is a whole-body tragedy, an integral human event of enormous proportions with massive repercussions."
>
> — Susan Pease Banitt

The traumatic nature of the event you experienced as well as your thoughts and feelings about what happened (and most of all, *how* it happened) color every aspect of the grief that follows. In other words, the traumatic event itself is part of your grief. But it is not the totality of your grief. As I've said, traumatic events create a unique, two-part grief experience: one focused on the event itself and one focused on the primary and secondary losses the event caused.

I propose that the term "traumatic grief" actually captures better than the term "PTSD" or even "post-traumatic stress" the totality of people's experience following a traumatic event. "PTSD" is all about the event of the loss, whereas "traumatic grief" acknowledges both the traumatic event itself and the entirety of the grief journey that follows.

> "Some people's lives seem to flow in a narrative; mine had many stops and starts. That's what trauma does. It interrupts the plot. You can't process it because it doesn't fit with what came before or what comes afterwards."
>
> — Jessica Stern

While PTSD thinking assumes that the moments of the traumatic event are what matters most, traumatic-grief thinking understands that the traumatic event set an entire grief cascade in motion, one that includes an array of primary and secondary losses. Focusing on PTSD to the exclusion of grief is like having a triple-bypass for coronary artery disease without also changing your diet and exercise habits (not to mention never processing your emotional, social, and spiritual thoughts and feelings about the event of the surgery). Yes, open-heart surgery may "fix" the immediate, life-threatening symptoms, but unless it is followed by more holistic care and self-care, your overall health and well-being will not improve. The same can be said for PTSD treatment that does not also focus on the broader traumatic grief landscape.

Please allow me one more word about the diagnosis and term PTSD. As a clinician who has counseled many people in grief over the last four decades, I myself am well aware of the usefulness of diagnostic codes and "labels." In our current healthcare climate, being diagnosed with PTSD or another mental illness opens the doorway to treatment. If your caregiver doesn't provide a diagnostic code, your insurance company will not pay for your treatment. And most people do not have the resources to pay for ongoing therapy or treatment on their own.

What's more, the label "PTSD" is in essence a handle that allows our culture and our caregivers to grab hold of and talk about the issue. We are witnessing the brokenness of millions among us—you included—so we created a shorthand term that enables us to talk to one another about what we are seeing or experiencing. So, while I strongly believe that the term PTSD is flawed, perhaps for now, at least, it is also serving an essential purpose.

Traumatic grief as a form of complicated grief

Again, grief is the sum total of all the thoughts and feelings you experience when you lose something or someone of great value to you. Grief is normal, natural, and necessary after a loss. In the next chapter I will talk more about mourning, which is the equally essential outward expression of your grief.

Some grief caregivers refer to the process of open, active, and communicative grief and mourning as "good" grief. Good grief creates conditions for the healthy integration of loss and fosters good mental health. Good, or "uncomplicated," grief is essentially grief that slowly, over time and with the support of others, softens as it is expressed and worked through.

CARE-ELICITING SYMPTOMS

I want you to understand that the symptoms of grief, uncomplicated or complicated, typical or traumatic, are care-eliciting symptoms. They are not signs of illness but rather symptoms of an injury that needs careful and compassionate tending. They are signs that let you and others know that you need care. So if you are experiencing symptoms that are not softening, no matter what they are or how severe or mild they may be, that means you need more care and self-care.

Complicated grief, on the other hand, is grief that has gotten "stuck" or "off track" for some reason. When grief strays off course in this manner, it can go on and on without ever softening or without the grieving person ever reaching reconciliation. And as in the case of PTSD, certain parts of the grief experience can become so prominent and stuck that they may take over the griever's life.

Some people who experience a traumatic event seem to heal without their grief ever incapacitating them. They keep handling their daily tasks of living. They continue to maintain loving relationships. As we said earlier, it is thought that about 15 percent of people affected by a traumatic event go on to develop diagnosable PTSD. They are the people whose grief is clearly stuck or off track. They are the people whose grief has become what I call "complicated." Perhaps you are among them. The remaining 85 percent presumably find ways to work through their two-part traumatic grief without being overtaken by crippling symptoms. (Though some of this 85 percent are surely hiding, or carrying, their grief. See page 99.)

Traumatic loss circumstances are one significant risk factor for the development of complicated grief, but there are others, as well. The more risk factors you have, the more likely you are to find yourself in PTSD or complicated-grief territory after a traumatic event.

Ten risk factors for complicated grief

How many of these might pertain to your traumatic grief?

1. *The specific circumstances of the loss*

    A traumatic event is a dramatic example of loss circumstances
    that can complicate grief. The event is typically but not always
    sudden and/or unexpected. It is also usually violent. We've
    already discussed what could be considered a "traumatic"
    loss, but here I would like you to also consider that the
    traumatic loss event may include circumstances that even in
    untraumatic situations could complicate grief, such as

    - out-of-order deaths or injuries (physical or spiritual).
      Whenever children or younger people are affected, we
      instinctively feel that the loss is a tragedy and very, very
      wrong.

    - uncertainty surrounding the loss. When it's unclear why
      an event happened or who may have been at fault, when
      information about the loss is withheld, or when a traumatic
      event kills people but their bodies are mutilated and so can't
      be viewed by grievers or the bodies are simply irrecoverable/
      missing, grief is often complicated.

    - the griever's sense of responsibility. Guilt often complicates
      grief in circumstances such as car accidents and wartime
      traumas (people in the military often feel that as "warriors"
      they should have been able to prevent the death of a fellow
      service member), but it also arises in more natural loss
      situations, such as illnesses in which grievers feel they may
      have made poor medical decisions or divorces in which one
      or both parties feels unbearably responsible.

2. *Your personality, including the ability to understand and access emotions (emotional intelligence)*

People who struggle with self-sufficiency in general often struggle with how to navigate in the aftermath of loss. Those with a history of difficulty integrating grief/loss into their lives are more at risk for complicated grief whenever a new loss arises. Also, complicated grief is more common in people who tend to form ambivalent, conflicted, or abusive relationships. These tendencies are often, but not always, a family-of-origin issue.

Likewise, people who deny or "stuff" their emotions—consciously ("I don't need to cry/get all emotional") or unconsciously—can easily experience complicated grief. Some of these people also have a tendency to intellectualize or try to "manage" their losses and may seem to be holding it together on the outside, but are often, on the inside, struggling with feelings of emptiness, anger, hypersensitivity, and other dark emotions.

In traumatic grief, "loss overload" can hamper both people's usual resilience and emotional intelligence. After experiencing a traumatic event, people who were formerly self-sufficient and effectively emotional can sometimes, understandably, no longer process their thoughts and feelings. The magnitude of the event, or their internal response to it, is too great for them to thrive using their former coping skills alone. If you seem to have experienced a change in personality and/or emotional resilience after the traumatic event, this is a sign that your grief has become complicated and you need additional support.

3. *In the case of the death of someone loved, your relationship with the person who died*

While this is only sometimes a factor in traumatic grief, I am including it here because it is often a contributor to complicated grief. People who have unreconciled conflict with or ambivalence toward a loved one who dies traumatically commonly run into challenges in their grief. The rockiness often stems from a history of abuse, intermittent break-ups in the relationship, mental health issues, drug or alcohol abuse, and/or codependence emotionally, physically, or financially.

4. *Your access to and use of support systems*

People who are alone in life—no partner (or an uncommunicative partner), no friends, no close colleagues— are at risk for complicated grief because grief demands the ongoing support of others.

Traumatized grievers, especially, need social support and often specialized social support. Their grief experience is naturally complicated by the traumatic nature of the loss, and they need the ongoing compassion and understanding of people who have gone through a similar experience and/or are trained to create a safe place for their intense symptoms to be expressed.

Of course, those whose personalities preclude them from seeking or accepting such support (see number 2) are at risk for complicated grief, as are those whose support systems judge their grief as abnormal or encourage them to just "get over it" and "move on."

5. *Your cultural/ethnic background*

   Some cultures are better at embracing emotionality and loss than others. When you grow up in a culture that treats grief and loss as "something we don't talk about," you yourself are likely to judge your own feelings of grief as abnormal and wrong. In general, North Americans tend to be emotion-phobic, which is a drastic mismatch for the traumatized griever. An extreme example is the treatment of Vietnam veterans after the war. Traumatized by their experience, they came home to a culture that not only scorned their normal and necessary grief but blamed them for its causes.

6. *Your religious/spiritual/philosophical background and current worldview*

   As with cultural background, the griever's religious background can complicate grief. Some faiths overtly make the claim that if you are a strong believer, you do not need to grieve and mourn because a) God does everything for a reason (and you don't need to understand His reasons) and b) this trouble-filled life on Earth is only temporary and is followed by an everlasting life of joy.

   While many clergy members are excellent helpers, sometimes traumatized grievers turn to or are sent to prescriptive clergy people, who in turn tell the griever how to think and behave in the aftermath of a loss. This is insidiously harmful. Any "support" grievers receive that does not witness and accept them as they are but rather dictates what is right and wrong can contribute to complicated mourning.

7. *Other stressors in your life*

   The number and magnitude of other stressors in grievers' lives can easily complicate their grief. A history of mental health challenges, such as depression or anxiety, often worsens those symptoms in normal grief and can really magnify them in traumatic grief. Other stressors, such as compromised health and financial challenges, can also complicate grief.

Traumatic grief often stems from an event that itself created multiple losses, or stressors. Many people might have died or been injured. Homes and belongings may have been destroyed. Add these on top of other, more common stressors in the griever's life (an aging parent, young children who require constant care, normal bills) and you definitely have a recipe for complicated grief.

8. *Your upbringing and unwritten family rules*

Children learn how to express or inhibit emotions from their parents and other close family members and usually grow up to be adults who follow suit. Grievers from a "closed" family system are more likely to deny, repress, convert, or avoid the need to mourn. Other family challenges, such as a history of rocky or codependent relationships, can contribute to complicated grief, especially when a traumatic event is involved.

9. *Your participation in meaningful rituals*

Throughout all of history and across all cultures, humans have turned to ritual to mark important life transitions and process thoughts and feelings too profound to handle in everyday conversations and routines. After a death, for example, the funeral helps grievers acknowledge and begin to embrace the painful reality of the loss. It also provides a culturally sanctioned time and place for grievers to support one another. I often say that a meaningful funeral assists with reality, recall, support, expression, meaning, and transcendence.

In the aftermath of a traumatic event, rituals can also be extremely helpful to grievers. That is why ceremonies long after the event continue to be held at Ground Zero and other trauma sites. In my own practice, I use a minimum of three ceremonies, spread out over time, with anyone I counsel for traumatic grief. From simple candle-lighting rituals (in which the griever lights one candle representing each of his most prominent feelings about the trauma, honoring and embracing each feeling as he talks about it), to releasing balloons or sky lanterns that represent various aspects of the traumatic experience, to creating and ritually using a small shrine in honor of the many losses caused by the trauma, such ceremonies accommodate traumatic grief in ways nothing else can.

Grievers whose loss is not recognized by ritual, on the other hand, or who choose not to or cannot (because of distance, for example) participate in such rituals are at risk for complicated grief because sometimes only ritual is "big" enough to give shape to what happened. Of course, for some traumatized grievers, such as rape victims, public ceremony is not appropriate or forthcoming. For these people, more intimate, customized rituals in the context of a support group or even individual counseling is a way to tap into the power of ceremony as a therapeutic tool.

10. Losses that tend to be stigmatized

Certain loss circumstances tend to be stigmatized, such as suicide, homicide, death by certain illnesses (such as AIDS), perinatal loss, same-sex loss, and, of course, PTSD.

These types of losses are typically not openly acknowledged, publicly mourned, or socially supported. The people who experience such losses naturally grieve inside, but because there is a social stigma surrounding the nature of the loss, they are at greater risk for what is called "disenfranchised grief." Social support is often lacking, and not uncommonly, the griever's sense of culturally instilled shame makes them question the legitimacy of their grief and their right to openly mourn.

Other kinds of losses that may fit in this category are not stigmatized so much as overlooked or minimized, such as the death of an older adult, ex-spouse, or coworker. These circumstances can also create disenfranchised and thus complicated grief.

What complicated grief can look like

I believe that PTSD is a form of complicated grief. It is grief that has become "stuck" or "off track" because of the traumatic nature of the circumstances that caused it in addition to, in many cases, some combination of the other risk factors listed above.

We've already reviewed the diagnostic symptoms of PTSD, and if you're reading this book, you probably have extensive personal experience with what it looks and feels like to live with PTSD. So PTSD is likely what *your* complicated grief looks like. Below I've listed some other common symptoms of complicated grief. If you recognize yourself in any of them, it simply means that you should consider the additional symptoms part of your complicated grief, as well.

Absent or delayed grief

Absent or delayed grief is grief that seems to be nonexistent. When someone experiences a loss but is not given the opportunity (or does not perceive a need) to mourn, or is stuck in shock or denial, grief may seem to be absent but is only, in fact, delayed or "carried." (See page 99.) Of course, after a significant loss, denial is normal and necessary for a short time during those early days of shock and numbness, but ongoing denial or postponement is harmful and a sign of complicated grief.

In many situations, PTSD is a form of delayed grief. For example, in the military, if a service member next to you is killed, you don't lay your gun down in order to mourn. You are actually trained to keep fighting. Months or sometimes years later you return home. Now safe, you begin to have symptoms that reflect the need for what I call "catch-up mourning" (see page 107). Depending on your complete symptoms picture, it is only long after the event that you may be labeled with PTSD.

Distorted grief

Distorted grief is grief that seems to focus on one particular thought or feeling. Instead of the symptoms softening, it hardens and gets locked in place—thus it is distorted and covers up underlying emotions like hurt, pain, fear, and helplessness. If someone who has experienced a significant loss is extremely angry all the time, to the exclusion of other grief feelings, for example, I would suspect complicated grief. I also often see distorted grief expressing itself as depression (where the normal and necessary sadness of grief becomes clinical depression), guilt (where the person self-punishes), or acute anxiety (where symptoms such as panic attacks and hyper-arousal dominate).

Converted grief

Converted grief can have a number of appearances. One is grief in which the intense feelings of loss are displaced or directed at other situations or people. For example, some grievers with converted grief begin to have trouble at work or in relationships with other people. They may feel depressed, bitter, and hateful, yet are unaware that those feelings are, in actuality, tied to their loss.

Other times converted grief is replaced. If the griever takes the emotions that were invested in a relationship that ended in death, for example, and reinvests them prematurely in another relationship, he may be attempting to replace his grief. This replacement pattern does not only occur with other relationships, but with other life activities as well. For example, he may become a workaholic although he has never been one in the past.

Sometimes converters minimize or intellectualize their grief. If they are aware of their feelings of grief but try to downplay them, or if they try to prove to themselves that the loss doesn't affect them very much, they may be minimizing their grief. Or they may talk openly about how "well they are doing" and how "their life is back to normal," even though the loss is recent.

> "Pain is a pesky part of being human."
>
> — C. JoyBell C.

Finally, some converters somaticize their grief by converting their emotions into physical symptoms. Grievers can become so completely preoccupied with their physical problems that they have little or no energy to relate to other people or do their work of mourning.

Other converters exchange their grief for addictive behaviors. Many abuse drugs or alcohol, but others become addicted to exercise, shopping, sex, gambling, or other repetitive physical actions. This is a very common symptom of complicated grief— one that merits the assistance of a skilled and compassionate grief counselor.

Chronic grief

In chronic grief, grievers experience acute symptoms of grief (inability to experience pleasure, confusion, difficulty focusing, lethargy, and others) that do not change or soften over time. Chronic grief tends to be globalized. That is, no one symptom of grief is dominant, as it is in distorted grief. Rather, the griever continues to actively mourn and seems to place all her energies on the loss. In traumatized grief, you might see this in people who devote their entire lives to the "cause" of the trauma to the exclusion of other interests, people, and opportunities.

You might be able to think of other factors that can turn good grief into complicated grief. In the context of PTSD, certainly the traumatic nature of the event alone is enough to complicate your grief, but when you are considering how your own grief may have become complicated, I urge you to consider the other complicated grief presentations listed above as well.

By the way, instead of "complicated grief," the DSM uses the term "Persistent Complex Bereavement Disorder" to describe intense grief that continues to prevent a person from functioning a year or more after a death. No matter what you call it, complicated grief is grief that has somehow been pulled off the path and needs to find its way back to it.

Everyone who experiences a trauma suffers traumatic grief. In other words, grief caused by a trauma *is* traumatic grief. The trauma alone and/or the trauma in combination with the risk factors mentioned in this chapter may complicate their grief. It may turn their normal and necessary grief into a form of complicated grief that is commonly called PTSD. To me, what this all boils down to is that the traumatic nature of a loss is one of many risk factors for complicated grief. But whether or not the person ends up with a diagnosis of PTSD, traumatic grief, complicated grief, or persistent complex bereavement disorder doesn't matter at all compared to the truly important questions:

How can we help the millions of people struggling with the disabling symptoms of PTSD?

How can we help you, especially if other treatments haven't been working?

And maybe most important of all, how can you help yourself truly and deeply heal?

The answers to these questions are the subject of the next chapter.

PART THREE

MOURNING AS "TREATMENT"

We've been talking a lot about the symptoms of uncomplicated grief, traumatic grief, complicated grief, and PTSD. Basically, when you add all the symptoms together, you get the experience we call "grief." Grief is the totality of everything you think and feel inside after a loss.

Mourning is the outward expression of that grief. And mourning, I firmly believe and have observed time and time again, is the key to healing.

"Give sorrow words; the grief that does not speak whispers the o'er-fraught heart and bids it break."

— William Shakespeare

Mourning is treatment, if you will. People who suffer from PTSD may also need simultaneous medical treatment, such as drug therapy, but because your symptoms are, in essence, caused by loss, there is no getting around the fact that mourning is *the* essential work of your often long and arduous journey back to well-being.

"Grief is itself a medicine."

— William Cowper

Mourning, as I stated in the Introduction, is the missing piece to the puzzle of healing PTSD.

I'd like to point out here that I don't usually use the word "treatment" when it comes to grief. To treat, which literally means "to drag," implies that grief is a disease that must be cured. But as I have emphasized, grief is definitely not a disease. It is the normal and necessary response to an injury caused by significant loss.

But because PTSD or traumatic grief is thought of as a medical condition by many, I am using the word treatment here to emphasize that no matter which combination of therapeutic approaches you might be prescribed or you might try, mourning is always, always essential.

Have you noticed that most PTSD treatments encourage you to hurry up and "recover from" your psychic injuries? Pain and feelings of loss are seen as something to prevent or get beyond as soon as possible. Yet here is the secret:

Just as after a serious bodily injury, healing a serious psychic injury takes as long as it takes. We can and must actively work toward healing, but we cannot hurry the process, nor can we avoid the pain.

Traumatic loss changes people's lives forever. And the movement from "before" to "after" is a naturally long, painful journey. The injury caused by a traumatic event requires a time of *convalescence*…a very slow, gradual return to health.

So yes, it takes time, but it also takes work. Contrary to what we sometimes believe, time alone does not heal all wounds. From my own experiences with both traumatic and normal grief as well as those of the thousands of grieving people I have companioned over the years, I have learned that if we are to integrate loss into our lives, we cannot skirt the outside edges of our grief. Instead, we must journey all through it, sometimes meandering the side roads, sometimes plowing directly into its raw center. We must experience it, and then we must express it.

First, seek safety and comfort

After a traumatic event, it's natural to feel vulnerable, unsafe, and anxious. You may even be experiencing disturbing panic attacks, hallucinations, or flashbacks. Your body's instinctive fight-or-flight response kicked in but may never have turned off or may have become injured. We've gone over the biochemistry of why and how these symptoms happen and sometimes linger, but we haven't yet discussed what to do about them.

> "Safety is something that happens between your ears, not something you hold in your hands."
>
> — Jeff Cooper

First, it's critical for you to understand that your first priority must be to find ways to feel safe. Unless and until you feel safe and have tamed your anxiety and fear enough that you can function in your daily life again, you won't be able to effectively and actively work on your six needs of mourning (we'll talk about those next).

Locating yourself among people and in places that make you feel safe is a good first step. If this means moving in with a friend or relative temporarily, that's OK. If this means avoiding certain places or people for now, that's OK, too.

Certain medical therapies may also help ease your fear-based symptoms. Anti-anxiety medication may be appropriate for you right now. Psychotherapies such as cognitive behavioral therapy can be useful in providing you with tools and techniques for redirecting your fearful thoughts and calming yourself. Complementary therapies such as yoga, hypnosis, and meditation groups may also be effective in helping make your fear and anxiety less controlling.

Also pay attention to what calms and comforts you. Taking a walk? Cuddling with someone you love? Hugging your pet? Relaxing in the tub? Reading or prayer? Meditation? Identify activities that soothe you and turn to them whenever your anxiety is high.

And if people who love you are available and willing to take care of you or help you with essential tasks when you are struggling with fear-based symptoms, please let them. You will not be able to harness the healing power of mourning if you feel unsafe or overly anxious. Seek safety and comfort first, then you can begin to slowly embrace your grief. Sometimes you may even need the assistance of a trained caregiver to help you do what is referred to as "trauma processing."

Your grief in action: mourning

Mourning is the active part of the traumatic grief journey. Much like active and ongoing wound care and physical therapy heal bodily injuries, mourning heals psychic injuries.

> "That I was only beginning the process of mourning did not occur to me. Until now, I had only been able to grieve, not mourn. Grief was passive. Grief happened. Mourning, the act of dealing with grief, required attention."
>
> — Joan Didion

If we don't acknowledge PTSD for what it really is—a grief response following a traumatic event—we actually end up building walls around the unhealed wound in an effort to protect it. But grief is the essence of PTSD. If we continue to ignore this truth, people like you will not receive adequate care and thus will continue to carry unhealed wounds.

In many ways, mourning is a series of spiritual awakenings borne of the willingness to have an authentic encounter with the pain surrounding the loss. Your PTSD treatment so far may well have been trying to "treat away" or help you go around your symptoms when what you actually need is help discovering the courage to surrender to the pain.

The medical model of PTSD care has placed the focus on selective symptoms relief. While I agree that the first thing people with PTSD often need is relief from their dramatic fear-based symptoms, which are often preventing them from functioning in their daily lives, these symptoms are only the tip of the iceberg that is their life-altering traumatic grief injury.

When we as humans experience trauma, we need to actively mourn in order to integrate into our lives the many losses caused by the traumatic event. This is difficult to do when feelings of grief are perceived as weakness in our "buck-up" culture. Traumatic grief then becomes something to be resolved and overcome rather than experienced.

But to be experienced and expressed is what it needs. To facilitate its expression—or mourning—a helpful concept is that of the six central needs of mourning. Your awareness of these needs can help you take on a more active role in working through your symptoms instead of considering them something you must passively endure or need to have treated away.

Before we jump into the six needs of mourning, I want to emphasize that as a traumatized griever who has been diagnosed with or relates to the concept of PTSD, you are experiencing grief that is naturally complicated. You will need the ongoing support of a compassionate therapist as you work through these needs. (For more on finding a good counselor, see page 84.)

THE SIX CENTRAL NEEDS OF MOURNING

1. Acknowledge the reality of what happened as well as the losses it created
2. Feel the pain of the losses
3. Remember the event
4. Develop a new self-identity
5. Search for meaning
6. Receive and accept ongoing help from others

Mourning Need 1: *Acknowledge the reality of what happened as well as the losses it created*

This need of mourning involves confronting the reality that the traumatic event happened and that it created a number of primary and secondary losses. I have found that acknowledging the full reality of the losses may take weeks, months, and sometimes even years. As humans, we can know something in our heads fairly quickly, but it can take much, much longer for us to fully embrace the reality in our hearts.

Especially in cases of traumatic grief, you may try to push away the reality of what happened at times. It's natural to want to protest the reality of the horrific event and the devastation it created. Some degree of denial, especially in the early, shock-filled days following the event, is a healthy coping mechanism. In fact, traumatic events often result in acute shock, or "psychic numbing." In other words, you may feel so deeply numb and in shock that it may take you a long time to emerge from this initial cocoon of protection. That is normal and necessary. It will take as long as it takes.

Over time, however, you must very slowly, gently, and with the support of others allow the reality into your head and heart. You

MOURNING AS "TREATMENT"

may find yourself moving back and forth between protesting and encountering the reality of the event and the losses that cascaded from it. You may do what I call the evade-encounter dance. You hide from it, then you allow yourself to encounter it briefly, then you hide from it again. This is also a normal protective mechanism.

> "Face reality as it is, not as it was or as you wish it to be."
>
> — Jack Welch

You may discover the need to replay the event over and over and confront memories, both good and bad. This replay is a vital part of this need of mourning. It is as if each time you talk it out, the traumatic event and the losses it created are a little more real and ultimately a little more manageable.

Of course, I understand that this need of mourning can be exceptionally difficult for people who have experienced a traumatic event. And acknowledging the reality in your own mind and heart is one thing: acknowledging it outside of yourself, which is what this mourning need requires, is another. My best advice is to take it slow, one bit at a time. Figure out who the good listeners are in your life and slowly—and over time—open up to them. You may well find that your family and friends are not able to help you with this difficult mourning need, so I encourage you to to consider working with a trained and compassionate counselor. In addition to talking it through, you may also want to write about it in a private journal or consider sharing anonymously in an online forum.

We as humans come equipped with an organic capacity to slowly integrate loss into our lives. We can embrace grief and allow it to unfold into mourning. The fact that we as humans are born instinctively knowing how to mourn tells us we are meant to gently acknowledge losses and integrate them into our lives. However, we cannot do this alone; we need the support of compassionate friends, family members, and caregivers.

IDEAS FOR MEETING MOURNING NEED 1:

Talk to people who care about you. Talk to others who experienced the same or a similar traumatic event. Participate in a support group. Journal about what happened. Allow for moments of denial and distraction, but don't allow yourself to go on denying and distracting indefinitely.

Mourning Need 2: *Feel the pain of the losses*

Did you know that to be "bereaved" literally means "to be torn apart"? When you are torn apart by traumatic loss, mourning requires embracing the pain of the losses. Yes, embracing. Befriending. Even wallowing in.

> "You care so much you feel as though you will bleed to death with the pain of it."
>
> — J.K. Rowling

For many people in our emotion-phobic, mourning-avoidant culture, it is easier to avoid, repress, or deny the pain of grief than it is to confront it. Yet, it is in confronting our pain, being honest about that pain, and realizing it doesn't mean something is wrong or "pathological" that we ultimately integrate loss into our lives.

CLEAN PAIN VERSUS DIRTY PAIN

"Clean pain" is the normal pain that follows difficult life experiences. "Dirty pain" is the damaging, multiplied pain we create when we catastrophize, judge ourselves, or allow ourselves to be judged by others. Dirty pain is the story we tell ourselves about the clean pain.

When someone we love dies, for example, we naturally experience grief. That is clean pain. But when we become frozen by worry that we did something wrong, or when we assume that others think badly of us (when in fact we don't really know what they think), or when we feel like we "should" be doing something differently than we are, we're experiencing dirty pain.

In your struggle with traumatic grief, dirty pain may be a complicating factor. A compassionate grief counselor can help you explore any dirty pain you might be experiencing and mourn your clean pain.

In many Eastern cultures, aging, illness, death, and grief are understood differently. When people live in daily contact with these realities, they tend not to deny that life involves pain and suffering. As Western culture has gained the capacity to limit pain and suffering, we tend to encourage the denial of pain.

Advances in medicine and ever-increasing technology to lengthen lifespans have, without doubt, improved the levels of physical comfort for many North Americans.

However—this is when a shift in perception seems to have taken place—as pain and suffering have become less visible or relegated to behind closed doors, they are no longer perceived as an intrinsic part of the nature of being human, but instead seen as a sign that something has gone wrong.

Through no fault of your own, you may have come to misunderstand the role of pain and suffering. If you openly express your painful feelings, misinformed friends and family members may advise you to "keep your chin up" or "let go." If, on the other hand, you remain "strong" and "in control," you may well be congratulated for "doing well" with your grief.

> "To share your weakness is to make yourself vulnerable; to make yourself vulnerable is to show your strength."
>
> — Criss Jami

Keep in mind that many friends and family members (and sometimes even caregivers) want you to stay in control as a form of self-protection. There are times when all of us attempt to control because we are *afraid* of the pain of grief. It hurts to embrace the depths of the loss. It hurts to acknowledge that life is often dangerous, mean, and capricious and to be humbled by our traumatic experiences and life losses.

But the hurt is the Truth with a capital T. It is a significant, unavoidable part of the human condition, and learning to embrace the hurt just as we embrace the joy and love is the key— at its most fundamental, the PTSD solution.

"Wait a minute...," participants in my workshops sometimes protest. "Are you saying it's really OK for people to wallow in their grief? To feel nothing but sorry for themselves?" Let's discuss that for a minute. One meaning of "wallow" is "to lie or roll in." Hippos instinctively wallow in the mud. Goats instinctively wallow in the dirt and dust. The animals naturally behave in this way because wallowing cools their body temperature and cleans them off. It's refreshing.

Conversely, we as a culture have come to believe that wallowing in our sorrow and pain is bad for us. But this understanding is a product of our grief-avoidance. It makes us uncomfortable to see others immersed in their pain, so we have appropriated the term "wallow" to describe emotionality and given it a negative connotation.

In fact, wallowing is *good*. After a significant loss, we instinctively and naturally withdraw and sit in the wound of our grief. If we are being honest with ourselves, saying hello to our grief and befriending the darkness, we lie in our pain. We roll in it. And ultimately, our wallowing refreshes us.

MOURNING AS "TREATMENT"

So yes, it really is OK—necessary even—for you to wallow in your grief for a time. Wallowing happens in liminal space—the time betwixt and between.

Like the winding of a spring or the crouch before a leap, it is the necessary pause that gives momentum to the coming forward movement.

CHRONIC WALLOWING

I would be remiss here if I did not also point out that some people wallow in their grief without ever finding a way to climb out. They take on the long-term persona of the griever or victim. They become, in essence and usually unknowingly, masochists to their grief.

We've talked about "complicated grief," which means grief that has become stuck or derailed in some way, and I've mentioned that chronic grief is one form of complicated grief. In chronic grief, grievers experience acute symptoms of grief (inability to experience pleasure, confusion, difficulty focusing, lethargy) that do not change or soften over time.

Have you ever known people who, in the aftermath of a significant loss, were forever depressed or lifeless? Who cocooned themselves in their loss and never emerged? This is what chronic grief looks like, and what it means is that the chronic griever needs help emerging from the darkness. He is stuck. He cannot see the forest for the trees. He runs the very real risk of dying while he is alive. He may have done a very good job of feeling the pain of the losses, but now he needs help emerging from that pain. He may be clinically depressed. He almost certainly needs the support of a compassionate therapist who has experience working with people in depression and grief.

If you are appropriately and constructively wallowing in the pain of your grief, you deserve congratulations. Befriending the darkness of grief takes courage and hard work. But if you find yourself stuck in the darkness, I hope you will muster the courage to get help. Do not be ashamed. You have done nothing wrong. You simply need a helping hand, as we all do at times. Counseling (and sometimes medication) can help you enter the light.

We feel pain and suffering in all five parts of our selves—physical, cognitive, emotional, social, and spiritual. We've already reviewed common symptoms of normal grief, but here let's look at how the symptoms may "show up" for you in each of these domains:

Physical: Grief naturally results in physical discomfort; your body responds to the stress of the encounter with symptoms such as headaches, muscle tightness, indigestion, and a compromised immune system, resulting in more colds and other viruses.

Cognitive: Grief naturally results in cognitive discomfort; thought processes are confused and memory is impaired.

Emotional: Grief naturally results in emotional discomfort, and a multitude of wave-like emotions may be experienced that demand comfort and care.

Social: Grief naturally results in social discomfort; you may withdraw, and/or friends and family may withdraw, and isolation may result.

Spiritual: Grief naturally results in spiritual discomfort; questions may arise such as "Why go on living?"; "Will my life have meaning?"; and "Where is God in this?"

Mourning Need 2 requires embracing all of these discomforts and pains.

The opposite of embracing pain is attempting to stay "in control." In fact, one way that people describe the sensation of PTSD is that they are "out of control." Underlying that controlling impulse is anxiety and fear—the lingering fear caused by the fight-or-flight response as well as the existential fear that you will have to experience even more pain in any or all of the five domains noted above.

In grief, out of control is where you are and where you need to be for a while. When you accept that you cannot go around the pain of what happened, you will discover the courage to relax into the pain, and therein lies the paradox. Trying to avoid, repress, or deny the pain of grief makes you an opponent of the journey and creates more chronic states of anxiety and depression.

> "Surrender is the intersection between acceptance and change."
>
> — Unknown

Control appears to be one of North Americans' favorite ways of running from grief and loss. We are so high on control that we think we can let go of control by simply wanting to. In other words, we think we can control relinquishing control! Human beings in grief do not let go of control: human beings in grief let go of the belief that we have control.

Spiritual maturity in grief is attained when you embrace a paradox—to live in the state of both encounter and surrender while simultaneously "working at" and "surrendering to" the journey As you come to know this paradox, you can, very slowly and with no rewards for speed, discover the soothing of your soul. In fact, many grievers have taught me that they actually find themselves wrapped in a gentle peace—the peace of living at once in the encounter (the "grief work") and the surrender (embracing the mystery of not understanding).

Understand, however, that you cannot (nor should you try to) overload yourself with the hurt all at one time. Mourning Need 2, like all the other mourning needs, usually takes years to meet, and even then it is never completely "finished." Give yourself time, and "dose" yourself with the pain. In fact, sometimes you may need to distract yourself from the pain of your losses, while at other times you will need to intentionally and courageously befriend the hurt. Dose the pain: yes! Deny or attempt to treat away the pain: no!

IDEAS FOR MEETING MOURNING NEED 2:

Allow yourself to cry openly whenever you need to. Talk about your pain. When your pain wells up and asks for your attention, stop what you are doing and sit with the pain. Write about it in your journal. Make artwork that expresses your feelings. Listen to music that stirs and allows you to access your emotions. Trust your therapist to support you as you both work at and surrender to your pain.

Mourning Need 3: *Remember the event*

In uncomplicated grief caused by death, grievers have a need to pursue a relationship of memory with the person who died. Instead of simply ending or forgetting about the relationship, which some medical-based grief models essentially advocate, what grievers actually need to do is convert the relationship from one of presence to one of memory. The love and attachment remain, but the focus of that love and attachment shift. (Grievers who believe that life continues after death, on the other hand, often shift their relationship from one of presence on Earth to one of presence separated, for the time being, by time and space.)

> "Even painful memories are ties that bind."
>
> — Milan Kundera

In traumatic grief, however, the need to remember is a controversial topic. Must you relive the events of the trauma in order to process and integrate the memories? Many, but not all, of the medical-model therapies for treatment of PTSD include an element of remembering. Exposure therapy, for example, as well as EMDR, focus on remembering and memory cues, and both have been found effective. Indeed, treatments that include some element of exposure therapy have proven the most powerful and reliable forms of treatment.

Techniques to conjure memories include, alone or in combination, imagining (silently, aloud, or in writing); *in vivo* (in person, real-life) exposure to places and situations that mimic the trauma; and technology-assisted (such as virtual reality). On the other hand, some PTSD treatment techniques, such as cognitive behavioral therapy, or CBT, may sometimes avoid memory-gathering and sharing altogether.

One issue with remembering the traumatic event that caused so many losses is that you may have gaps in your memory—those "hard drive" glitches we talked about earlier. The dissociative quality of the memory—that "it happened to someone else, not me" feeling—also can make the event hard, if not impossible, to remember. One interesting study showed that when we experience an event in virtual reality from our own point-of-view, we remember it well. But when we experience the event as an outside observer, we don't remember it well.

"The inability to get something out of your head is a signal that shouts, 'Don't forget to deal with this!' As long as you experience fear or pain with a memory or flashback, there is a lie attached that needs to be confronted. In each healing step, there is a truth to be gathered and a lie to discard."

— Christina Enevoldsen

Intrusive memories, of course, are also characteristic of PTSD. These are painful, often violent flashes of memory that arise unbidden and can hijack your brain, usually when you don't want them to. We might say these memories are part of the glitchy technology. But we might also say that they are memories asking to be expressed.

And finally, the PTSD research can't yet say definitively that memory processing is *essential* to healing. While treatments that include memory processing have resoundingly been found effective, others that haven't included memory processing, such as stress inoculation therapy, have also seemed helpful to some people.

So let's summarize what we know about remembering the traumatic event and its immediate aftermath and PTSD. Remembering the event as a component of treatment has been found effective. Sometimes with PTSD it may be impossible to remember some or all of the traumatic event itself. On the other hand, intrusive memories are also common. And finally, it's possible that memory processing as a means of effectively treating PTSD isn't absolutely necessary.

I've said that it's understandable to want to avoid both the reality and the pain of a loss but that acknowledging the loss and embracing the pain are essential to healing. It's also understandable for you to want to avoid your traumatic memories. And why not avoid them? We are all living in a culture that teaches us to move away from instead of toward our grief.

Yet, as with Mourning Needs 1 and 2, I believe that Mourning Need 3 is not entirely optional. As the famous Danish philosopher Søren Kierkegaard noted, "While life must be lived forward, it can only be understood backward."

Intentionally repressing or ignoring traumatic memories invites carried grief. It's like leaving a significant portion of a wound uncleansed and uncared for, on purpose. While all grief journeys are unique, and your particular needs and circumstances of course trump these generalizations, my understanding of PTSD as traumatic grief suggests that generally speaking, the conjuring and sharing of traumatic memories is usually necessary. To ignore painful or ambivalent memories is often to prevent true healing from taking place.

How much do you need to work to remember and share? A good rule of thumb is this: If it's something that's bothering you about what happened—giving you pain; often in your thoughts or dreams; making you feel ashamed, afraid, angry, or other strong emotions—take that as a sign that you need to encounter it and express it. As always with grief, the symptom is the thought or the feeling, and the path to healing is the expression of the symptom.

The good news is that remembering the past makes hoping for the future possible. The essence of finding meaning in the future is not to forget the past, but to embrace the past.

IDEAS FOR MEETING MOURNING NEED 3:

You may well need the support of a nonjudgmental, empathetic counselor as you work to revisit and share your traumatic memories. Try writing about your memories in a journal or talking about them in a support group, too, and see if those mourning methods help take some of your memories' power away. Always keep in mind, however, that remembering must be dosed. You cannot—nor should you try to—hurry through the remembering process or force yourself to tackle it before you are really ready. It takes time and patience.

Mourning Need 4: *Develop a new self-identity*

This need of mourning is almost always a big deal for people with PTSD. They typically describe themselves as being different now than they were before the traumatic event. They struggle with this change, often wanting to return to their previous selves. Is this true for you?

But of course, you are no longer the same person you were before the traumatic event. All of us are forever changed by the significant events in our lives, including loss. If I am diagnosed with cancer, for example, my self-concept shifts. I used to be healthy. Now I am unhealthy. I used to be invincible. Now I am vulnerable. I used to be a provider for my family. Now I may not be able to provide. At first these forced-upon-me changes in self-identity are painful because they are all losses. They feel like diminishments. Over time, as I integrate them into my being, though, I may find new opportunities for growth and joy sparkling in the rubble.

> "I know now that we never get over great losses; we absorb them, and they carve us into different, often kinder, creatures."
>
> — Gail Caldwell

Traumatic loss tends to force even more dramatic and painful changes in self-identity. After a roadside bomb detonates, the platoon leader who had always thought of himself as the protector of his unit must now come to terms with the reality that service members under his command have died. The woman who was raped must—slowly, over time, and with the compassionate support of her partner and other caring people in her life—reconstruct her sexuality. The mother of a teen who completed suicide must re-conceive what it means to be a mother. The ways all three of them define themselves and the ways in which others define them have changed.

MOURNING AS "TREATMENT"

Reconstitution of the self in the aftermath of a traumatic loss is a long, ongoing process, not a single event in time. You may find yourself feeling childlike as you struggle with your changing identity. You may exhibit a temporarily heightened dependence on others and experience feelings of helplessness, frustration, inadequacy, and fear. These feelings can be overwhelming and frightening, yet they are a natural response to this important need of mourning.

IDEAS FOR MEETING MOURNING NEED 4:

As always, talking to others will help you meet this mourning need. People who've been forced to undergo similar identity redefinition are often good sounding boards. They "get it." If you're someone who likes to read, you could also search for memoirs written by authors who've had similar life experiences. You might identify with their hard-won insights. Finally, share your role struggles with others affected by the same traumatic event—whether this is your family, neighbors, work colleagues, etc. Because they are part of the same "system," they will also be wrestling with their new or changed role within the system.

Mourning Need 5: *Search for meaning*

After a significant loss, we naturally question the meaning and purpose of life. We review our philosophy of life and explore religious and spiritual values as we work on this need. This need relates to renewing your rationale for life and living after it has been torn apart.

"Why" and "How" questions are common when you search for

> "All of us suffer some injuries from experiences that seem to have no rhyme or reason. We cannot understand or explain them. We may never know why some things happen in this life."
>
> — James E. Faust

meaning. "Why did this happen now, in this way?" "How will I go on living?" The "Why" questions often precede the "How" questions in this unfolding process. The search for a reason to go on living is a vital part of grief work that is usually missing from standard PTSD treatments and requires an expenditure of physical, emotional, and spiritual energy.

You may experience a profound lack of sense of direction or future purpose, particularly if your hopes, dreams, and plans for the future were invested heavily in people, places, or things damaged or destroyed in the traumatic event. At times, overwhelming sadness and loneliness may be your constant companions. After all, you are faced with finding some meaning in going on with life even though you may feel empty and alone.

Traumatic loss forces you to explore your worldview—that set of beliefs you have about how the universe functions and what place you, as an individual, occupy in that universe. Some studies have observed that people in modern Western culture tend to travel through life believing that the world is essentially a nice place in which to live, that life is mostly fair, and that they are basically good people who deserve to have good things happen to them. But when a traumatic event occurs, the pain and suffering that follow undermine these beliefs and can make it very difficult to continue living this happy life. Pain and suffering are often intensified as you try to reconstruct meaning in life.

So, where do you begin your search for meaning and renewal of resources for life and living? You might begin with your religious or spiritual traditions. Doubt may arise. For example, in the Judeo-Christian tradition, a foundational belief is that the universe was created by a good and just God. Traumatic events naturally challenge this belief in the goodness of God and the understanding that the world is essentially a nice place in which to live.

When such beliefs or longstanding worldviews are challenged in the early days and weeks after a traumatic event, there is often little, if anything, to replace them right away. This is a part of the "suspension" or "void" that grief creates—an absence of belief that must come before any renewal of belief. The void happens in liminal space. *Limina* is the Latin word for threshold. When you are in liminal space, you are not busily and unthinkingly going about your life. Neither are you living from a place of assuredness about your relationships and beliefs. Instead, you are unsettled. Both your mindless daily routines and your core beliefs have been shaken, forcing you to reconsider who you are, why you're here, and what life means.

Being in liminal space is frightening and unpleasant, but that's where traumatic grief takes you. Without loss (which you didn't ask for, by the way), you wouldn't go there. But here's the thing: it is only in liminal space that you can reconstruct your shattered worldview and re-emerge as a transformed, whole person who is ready to live fully again. If you think of your PTSD as, at least in part, an awful but necessary journey through liminal space—trusting that if you actively work on your six mourning needs while you're there, you will emerge into a safe, solid, and meaningful new life—perhaps the liminal experience will be more tolerable for you.

Bringing your torn-apart world back together takes time, loving companions, and humility—that virtue that helps us humans when we face powerlessness. The good news is that the need to openly mourn and the need to slowly discover renewed meaning in continued living can and do naturally blend into each other, with the former giving way to the latter as healing unfolds.

IDEAS FOR MEETING MOURNING NEED 5:
Schedule at least 15 minutes of "spirit time" into your routine each and every day; use this time to meditate, pray, read sacred

texts, take a walk in nature, or do any activity that makes you feel more in touch with the infinite and with God. Talk to a spiritual leader you respect. Read spiritual texts you find meaningful or uplifting. Attend a grief support group at your place of worship.

Of course, this suggestion also applies if you are struggling with or questioning God or your higher power. In this case, use your daily spiritual time to express your doubt or anger. Talk to a friend or spiritual leader about your disillusionment. Read spiritual texts that affirm and support your questioning. Spiritual time spent raging or questioning is still spiritual time. I often say, "Those who do not question do not find."

Mourning Need 6: *Receive and accept ongoing support from others*

This need acknowledges the reality that you need support long after the traumatic event. Because mourning is a "dosed" process that unfolds over time, you will need support and understanding for months and even years after the event. The quality and quantity of support you receive will be a major influence on your capacity to integrate the primary and secondary losses into your life and renew resources for living.

> "Neither refuse to give help when it is needed, nor refuse to accept it when it is offered."
>
> — Lloyd Alexander

Unfortunately, because our society places so much emphasis on returning to "normal" within a brief period of time, many grieving people are abandoned shortly after a traumatic event. Has this happened to you?

To be truly helpful, the people who make up your support system must appreciate the impact the event and all its fall-out losses have had and continue to have on you. They must understand that in order to slowly reconcile the losses, you must be allowed—even encouraged—to mourn long after the traumatic event. And they must perceive grief not as an enemy to be vanquished but as a necessity to be experienced.

You may or may not receive good support from individual family members or friends, from faith communities, or from other groups that are a part of you life. If the traumatic event you experienced carries a stigma (such as suicide, homicide, or rape), you may be finding that people you thought would be there for you are instead shying away. Often, the greater the stigma, the less the support available and the higher the risk for what is called "mutual pretense": when people around you know what has happened but believe they shouldn't bring it up.

The extreme nature of some PTSD symptoms can also make meeting this mourning need a challenge. If you have been experiencing flashbacks, panic attacks, or rage outbursts, for example, the people closest to you may have long since been scared away or feel as if their efforts are always rebuffed. The only way through this is with open, honest communication. In calmer moments, talk openly with the people who matter to you about your need for support—despite your sometimes off-putting behavior. Together establish ground rules about when and how they can best help you—and how to know when you need alone time.

You yourself may not be very good at openly seeking or accepting support. If you're not, this is something you can work on. You cannot get through this alone. Your PTSD is your unique struggle, it's true. But at the same time, if love and friendship are the most important things in your life (and I hope they are), your traumatic grief not only affects the people you care about, it can only be healed with their love and support. Remember that mourning is outward. It is grief gone public. Sharing your grief with the people who love you best is essential.

Obviously, certain days or times of the year will call out for extra-special support. For example, birthdays, holidays, the changing of seasons, and the anniversary of the event can all trigger what I call "griefbursts," which are heightened periods of grief and PTSD symptoms. Having others around or that you can rely on when a griefburst bursts in on you will help you through the darkest days.

IDEAS FOR MEETING MOURNING NEED 6:

Consider talking to the important people in your life one at a time about your traumatic grief. Having one-on-one, private conversations is less overwhelming than group meetings. Also work on saying "yes." Yes, I need your help. Yes, I am struggling. Yes, I have lost many things, and you are an important part of my finding my way back. In addition, support groups are often very helpful to traumatized grievers. Giving support to fellow travelers and receiving it in return in the safety of a bonded support group helps many traumatized grievers in a way that nothing else can. Professional counseling is also often necessary and transformative.

I cannot overemphasize the importance of these six needs of mourning. Essentially, actively working on them is the path to healing. It is your job and must be your priority.

Grief is real, and it does not simply go away as time passes. PTSD is a great example of the falsity of the adage, "Time heals all wounds." No, time alone does *not* heal severe psycho-spiritual wounds, any more than time alone could heal a badly broken arm or a clogged artery. Instead, PTSD requires active engagement with the six needs of mourning until symptoms begin to soften and fade into the background. Whenever a symptom arises, that means it's trying to get your attention. Giving it attention means mourning it—actively expressing it outside yourself through the six needs.

Finding a good counselor

While I do encourage you to seek help from a compassionate grief counselor, I must also warn you that still today, many therapists work from inappropriate assumptions about PTSD and the goals of counseling. Many continue to believe that PTSD is an illness that can and should be "cured." Few understand PTSD for what it really is—a form of complicated grief. Not long ago I wrote a book for caregivers called *Reframing PTSD as Traumatic Grief*, which has helped start the conversation in professional circles.

> "In therapy, the therapist acts as a container for what we daren't let out, because it is so scary, or what lets itself out every so often and lays waste to our lives."
>
> — Jeanette Winterson

You are not sick. There is nothing wrong with you. You will not "recover" from your traumatic grief. You will not "get over it." You will not achieve "closure." You will not be "cured." Instead, a truly helpful grief counselor, or "companion," will encourage you to tell and explore your story of trauma and loss. She will encourage you to explore the six central needs of mourning. She will help you find ways to feel safe and to function in the face of your PTSD, yes, but beyond that her main purpose will be to provide a safe place for you to mourn. She will bear witness to your pain. You will be the expert of your traumatic grief, and you will teach her what it is like for you. She will watch for signs that you need extra help with your fear-based symptoms, and in doing so, she will know if any biomedical treatment or trauma processing may be necessary in addition to the healing and transformative foundation of talk therapy.

THE POWER OF TELLING YOUR STORY

Traumatic experiences are as unique as snowflakes. Even two people who experienced the same traumatic event—same day, same time, same place—may have very different understandings, thoughts, and feelings about what happened. Part of your grief work now is to tell *your* unique story.

> "I now see how owning our story and loving ourselves through that process is the bravest thing that we will ever do."
>
> — Unknown

Although even the most empathetic listeners can never completely comprehend what you experienced, you will find comfort and support when you surround yourself with people who will honor your story of traumatic loss.

Find people who make you feel safe and will truly listen—who will let you share without trying to fix, take away, or distract you from what you are feeling. If talking about your story is difficult for you, take time to write it out and then share it with someone. Consider drawing or making something that represents what your grief journey feels like. Perhaps you can communicate your story through art instead of words with someone who is able to simply take in what you are communicating. Share your story in whatever ways feel natural to you.

Because the telling of and listening to stories of loss take time, patience, and unconditional love, they serve as powerful antidotes to a modern society that is all too often preoccupied with getting you to "let go," "move on," and "find closure." Whether you share your story with a friend, a family member, a coworker, or a fellow traveler in grief whom you've met through a support group, having others bear witness to the telling of your unique story is one way to go backward on the pathway to eventually going forward.

Honoring your one-of-a-kind story invites you to slow down, turn inward, and create the sacred space to do so. Having a place to have your story honored allows you to embrace what needs to be embraced and come to understand that you can and will come out of the dark and into the light. You heal yourself as you tell the tale. This is the awesome power of story.

Grief counselors who have been trained in my "companioning philosophy" of grief care understand and work from this point of view. Others sometimes naturally adopt this basic philosophy because they are good helpers and listeners, and they have learned over the years what really helps mourners heal and what does not. But too many therapists, tainted by the medical model of grief, which says that PTSD and even grief are illnesses that must be cured, still misunderstand their role in counseling traumatized grievers.

When you're interviewing counselors, here's a chart you might want to show to them that summarizes the difference between treating PTSD and companioning someone through PTSD:

TREATMENT MODEL IN PTSD	COMPANIONING MODEL IN PTSD
The patient is sick/has a disorder.	The traumatized griever is having a normal and necessary response to an abnormal reality.
Understanding the brain's biochemistry will lead us to a cure.	Traumatic grief inhabits the soul and is fundamentally a spiritual journey.
Positions the traumatized griever in a passive role—the "patient."	Positions the traumatized griever in an active role—the mourner.

Control or stop painful symptoms. Distress is bad.	Express the symptoms and seek to learn from them. Distress is necessary and ultimately beneficial.
Follows a prescriptive model in which the caregiver is the expert.	The grieving person guides the journey. "Teach me" is the foundational principle.
Establish control. Create strategic plan of intervention.	Show up with curiosity and willingness to learn from the griever.
Grieving person ranges from from compliant to non-compliant.	Grieving person expresses the reality of being "torn apart" as best he can.
Quality of care judged by how well the most obvious symptoms are "managed."	Quality of care monitored by how we allowed the griever to lead the journey and facilitated active mourning.
The goal is an outwardly functional individual.	The goal is an individual who feels a new sense of wholeness, meaning, and purpose from the inside out and who lives and loves fully as part of a family system.

And so, finding a good counselor to help you through your traumatic grief may take a little doing. A recommendation from someone you trust is probably the best place to start. If he or she had a good counseling experience and thinks you would work well with this counselor—especially if the counselor has experience helping people with PTSD, then you might want to start there.

Ultimately, though, only you will be able to determine if a particular counselor can help you. If a friend's recommendation doesn't work out, try more formal searching methods. Try asking a local bereavement group, which usually maintains a list of counselors specializing in grief therapy; your personal physician, who can often refer you to bereavement care specialists; or an information and referral service, such as a crisis intervention center, that maintains lists of counselors who focus on grief work.

Depending on the size and mental health resources of your community, you may want to seek out not just a good counselor but a good traumatic grief counselor. Someone skilled at marital counseling, for example, may have little or no understanding of traumatic grief issues. Search online for local counselors listing grief, bereavement, or PTSD as a specialty.

During your initial consultation with the counselor, ask the following questions:

- What are your credentials and where were you trained?
- Have you had specialized PTSD or traumatic grief training?
- What is your experience with grieving people?
- What is your counseling approach/recommended type of therapy with a grieving person?
- Do you have a medical consultant who assists you should I be a candidate for medication?

Again, I encourage you to choose a counselor who understands that traumatic grief is not an illness but a normal and necessary spiritual journey. If you end up seeing a therapist who tries to "cure" you or who doesn't believe that PTSD care must include talking about feelings and spiritual questions, it's time to find a new therapist.

Medical therapies for PTSD and how and when they support healthy mourning

Since PTSD was formalized as a diagnosis in the DSM-III in

1980, lots of scientific studies have been done and books written on the effectiveness of various forms of treatment. Because you may have already been treated with some of them and/or they may be proposed to you in the future, I'm going to briefly summarize the most widely used treatments below and offer my perspective on them through the lens of PTSD as traumatic grief.

Psychological debriefing

The concept of psychological debriefing in the aftermath of a traumatic event is based on the assumption that when people are given a structured, safe opportunity—not long after the event—to "download" their memories of what happened, as well as their thoughts and feelings about it, and to be assured that their thoughts and feelings are normal, they will be less likely to go on to develop PTSD. Debriefings can be conducted one-on-one, between a therapist and a griever, or in a group setting. Most are designed as single-session debriefings, though sometimes the debriefing might entail two or more meetings.

PTSD research seems to have concluded that psychological debriefings do not, in fact, prevent PTSD. My take on debriefings is that it is impossible to ever completely "release" one's thoughts and feelings about a traumatic event, let alone in a single meeting. Grief is a long-term journey—especially traumatic grief. And while good supportive care in the early hours and days of post-trauma shock is essential, no immediate therapeutic technique can preempt or "nip in the bud" the traumatic grief that will naturally, and essentially, unfold in the coming months and years.

Early cognitive behavioral interventions

Cognitive behavioral therapy (CBT) is a psychotherapeutic approach that teaches people affected by a traumatic event to use goal-oriented, systematic procedures when "dysfunctional" patterns of thoughts and feelings arise. Early post-trauma CBT has been used as an attempt to educate people in the use of redirecting techniques, so that when they are struggling with common thoughts and feelings in the months after the event, they will have self-correcting skills at their disposal. For example, if in thinking about what happened you tend to arrive at the belief, "It was my fault," CBT therapy might help you notice that thought when it arises and substitute it with something more positive and likely accurate, such as, "I didn't do anything wrong. Sometimes bad things just happen."

Early CBT with ongoing monitoring of symptoms can be effective, says the research, though researchers are still trying to pin down methods that will allow them to identify which victims need how much early CBT and monitoring.

To my way of thinking, early CBT is an attempt to force traumatized grievers to quickly rationalize or "think away" a profoundly spiritual injury before they've even had a chance to begin to plumb the depth and breadth of the injury. While I agree that trauma victims need support in the early days and weeks after the event, thinking-skills training is inadequate and, in fact, relying on it alone is detrimental to people's long-term well-being and self-actualization. To me, a central principle of healing traumatic grief is that caregivers must enter into what grievers think and feel without believing that their job is to *change* what grievers think and feel.

Short-term cognitive behavioral therapy
Many studies have been done on the effectiveness of various CBT techniques on PTSD, including exposure therapy, cognitive processing therapy, stress inoculation training, and others. The

course of treatment is typically short, ranging from six to 15 sessions of an hour or two each, once or twice a week. Usually the sessions are individual, but sometimes they are structured as group meetings.

Of the short-term therapies, the most widely studied has been exposure therapy, in which people are guided through re-imagining and describing the traumatic event and are often also physically exposed to low-risk places and activities that remind them of the traumatic experience. Exposure therapy often works, and I believe it is because it doses people with several of their natural needs of mourning (especially Needs 1, 2, 3, and 6; see pages 66 through 84). But still, while exposure therapy is indeed very helpful, it does not necessarily allow the traumatized person to lead the counseling session with what is, at any given moment, most pressing for her. What if today she is most struggling with the meaning of the event or her despair in trying to find a reason to go on?

Cognitive processing therapy (CPT), which involves the therapist helping people become overtly aware of their thoughts, feelings, and changed beliefs since the traumatic event and provides people with tools for "rethinking" those thoughts, feelings, and changed beliefs, has also been proven effective. As with exposure therapy, CPT doses people in several central mourning needs (especially 1, 2, 3, and 5). This is good. But it also runs the risk of essentially communicating to people that their thoughts and feelings are bad or unhealthy and that they simply need to think differently. "Don't think this…think that." That brand of judging and pathologizing does not affirm the normalcy of people's grief.

Stress inoculation training (SIT) also makes the Agency for Health Care Policy and Research's "A list" for treatment of

PTSD. In SIT, people are educated about healthy and unhealthy stress responses and taught new skills in emotion regulation, cognitive appraisal, problem-solving, communication, and socialization. During SIT sessions, people ostensibly talk about some of their trauma-related thoughts, feelings, and behaviors, but the focus is on helping replace them with new thoughts, feelings, and behaviors—ones that will help them "cope better." As with CPT, I fear that SIT, in essence, teaches people that their existing thoughts, feelings, and behaviors are "bad" and makes the therapist, rather than the griever, the expert of the grief experience.

Exposure therapy, CPT, SIT, and other forms of CBT likely deserve a place in the PTSD caregiving toolkit, but none of these techniques alone can provide sufficient care. Long-term, companioning-based talk therapy is the essential foundation.

Simply put, traumatized grievers need and deserve more holistic, soul-based care.

COMPLEMENTARY THERAPIES FOR TRAUMATIC GRIEF

I advocate a holistic approach to PTSD care. Any therapy that helps you with the six central needs of mourning and takes into account the fact that your grief affects you physically, cognitively, emotionally, socially, and spiritually may be an appropriate part of your care.

Many so-called "complementary" therapies fit the bill. My ironic quote marks stem from the fact that the medical establishment sees other forms of care as complementary—non-essential add-ons to their foundational and essential care—when in fact complementary therapies may be just as if not more essential to helping traumatized grievers than, say, drug therapy.

Yoga and reiki, for example, can help you with not only the physical symptoms of your grief but also your spiritual journey. Music therapy can assist with the accessing and expression of deep emotions. Hypnosis may be an avenue to unlocking authentic thoughts and feelings.

As you work on your six central needs of mourning, keep in mind that complementary therapies can and should be considered as tools for active mourning.

Drug therapy

Earlier I summarized the body's fight-or-flight response when it is exposed to a dangerous stressor, including the cascade of neurotransmitters and hormones that flood the body. I also discussed the understanding, gleaned from brain imaging, that in PTSD these biochemicals are likely wholly or in part responsible for the heightened, unyielding nature of the body's fear response—what people sometimes describe as the "I'm stuck in that terrible moment" quality of PTSD.

While prescription drugs have not yet been developed specifically to treat PTSD, medications commonly and effectively used to treat depression and other anxiety disorders, especially the class of anti-depressants called SSRIs and SNRIs, have been shown to ease PTSD symptoms that interfere with a person's ability to function in his day-to-day life and to participate in therapy.

I support the use of prescription medications, when indicated, as one element in a multifaceted approach to helping people who are suffering from PTSD. For one, fear-based symptoms that are so severe they prevent people from eating, sleeping, grooming, leaving the house, and other essential tasks must first be addressed before more emotional-spiritual repercussions can be considered. As I said earlier in this chapter, a sense of safety has to come first.

Similarly, symptoms that prevent people from attending therapy sessions or accepting any support from friends and family members can be eased by medication. While to some degree these symptoms are a normal part of traumatic grief in the short term, it is also necessary for them to soften, so that deeper, longer-term grief work can begin.

Still, despite studies that seem to confirm the effectiveness of certain medications in the treatment of PTSD, I urge extreme caution in their use. In some circles, for example, prescribing anti-anxiety medication, antidepressants, and antipsychotics to those struggling with PTSD or other mental health issues seems to be routine. But many of these people are not receiving simultaneous and ongoing talk therapy. Instead, they are being given drugs as a quick and convenient "solution" to their symptoms. The problem is, their symptoms are not strictly biochemical. They are also—actually, primarily—spiritual. Exposure to violence and atrocities creates deep psychic injuries that can't be fixed with a pill. First and foremost, traumatic grief requires the compassionate understanding and support of our fellow human beings.

> "Lord, help me become the person my psychiatrist medicates me to be."
>
> — Unknown

EMDR

Eye movement desensitization and reprocessing (EMDR) is a fascinating therapeutic technique that has been around since the 1980s. It's based on the belief that traumatic memories can remain stuck as "unprocessed memories," causing PTSD symptoms. Through a structured process of guiding the person to recall traumatic images, or mental pictures, usually together with back-and-forth eye or bodily movements, followed by a conjuring of positive mental images, the therapist helps the person process the negative images and replace them with positive ones.

Studies have resoundingly found EMDR effective in the treatment of PTSD.

While there are varying brain-biology-based theories as to why this might be so, it is generally believed that EMDR is a close cousin, or maybe even a twin, to exposure therapy.

Any therapeutic technique that encourages the exploration of traumatic memories in a safe, supportive environment gets my vote. While EMDR alone does not constitute an appropriately holistic treatment plan, it does appear that EMDR can be an effective component.

Psychosocial rehabilitation

Programs and treatment that focus on social and occupational functioning instead of symptoms management fall under the heading of psychosocial rehabilitation. This category includes things like patient education, social skills training, and case management. In essence, the goal is to help the person with PTSD become independent once again by retraining him to live, work, and communicate with others.

I'm sure that some PTSD sufferers, those whose psychic injuries are so severe that they cannot function at all, need and deserve the support that psychosocial rehabilitation offers. But first what they need and deserve is help mourning their grief. Without mourning, they will continue to live with and suffer from their profound injuries, even if the psychosocial rehabilitation helps them return to what may look, on the surface, like normal life.

A number of other treatments for PTSD have been used and formally studied, including dialectical behavior therapy, relaxation training, hypnosis, and more. If traumatic grief were a pie, I believe that the medical-model-based therapies can lay claim to slices—some skinny and some wide, but never the whole pie. They also tend to imply that the traumatic grief experience—the entire pie—is bad or wrong. In their pathologizing, they teach people who are suffering from awful symptoms that they are among the small percentage of people exposed to trauma who have developed "maladaptive responses" or an "illness" or a "disorder." In other words, the pie is bad.

But the pie's not bad. The pie is normal and necessary. Only the event that created the pie was bad.

PART FOUR

WHAT HAPPENS WHEN YOU DON'T MOURN YOUR TRAUMATIC GRIEF

Let's say you're one of the many millions of people the world over who has received some form(s) of treatment for your PTSD, yet you're still struggling. Maybe you continue to feel angry or depressed. Perhaps you feel hopeless or regretful. Maybe you haven't been able to re-establish strong, meaningful relationships in your life.

If you have ongoing symptoms that you can trace back, at least in part, to the traumatic event, you may well be suffering from what I call "carried grief."

"Revealing your feeling is the beginning of healing."

— Unknown

You see, when people carry their pain from life losses—when they keep it inside them instead of expressing it actively and fully through mourning—it comes back to haunt them. It keeps trying to get their attention until they give it the attention it demands and deserves.

When grief goes unexpressed, or unmourned, it destroys people's enthusiasm for life and living. It can deny them their creativity, gifts, and talents. The result is that these parts of themselves go stagnant or remain unclaimed inside of them, wanting to get out but feeling trapped. I often call it "living in the shadow of the ghosts of grief."

For traumatized grievers who have not been well companioned through mourning and who have not reconciled their traumatic loss experiences and subsequent grief fully, it is as if they have an imaginary cage surrounding them. In the cage are a multitude of potential symptoms that reveal that they are carrying the pain of grief. Trapped inside the cage, they are devoid of the desire to fulfill their life dreams, which is the very essence of creating a meaningful life and fulfilling their spiritual potential.

Symptoms of carried grief

Following are some of the common fall-out symptoms I have observed in people who are living in the shadow of the ghosts of grief—both uncomplicated grief and traumatic grief—and have not had the opportunity or willingness to authentically mourn. A culture that too often labels grief symptoms as pathological, that shames people for openly mourning life losses, that is preoccupied with quick fixes for emotional pain, invariably ends up inviting people to carry grief. So if you see yourself in the paragraphs that follow, do not feel ashamed. Our culture and perhaps some of the other risk factors listed on pages 49 through 55 have colluded to cause your carried grief.

Difficulties with trust and intimacy
People naturally fear what they do not know. I often think of how mourning requires a safe holding environment, a reliable sanctuary that is able to affirm all that we are and feel. When people experience loss but have not been provided with the safety and encouragement to mourn, their trust in people and the

world around them is naturally compromised. And so, they often fear intimacy and avoid closeness to others.

Many grief-carriers have taught me that they feel unlovable. Whether they attribute their self-esteem issues to unmourned losses or not, their brokenness makes them feel deficient or less-than. This can become, of course, a self-fulfilling prophecy. The grief-carrier may have an awareness of the need for love but at the same time feel unworthy of it. The reality is that this person feels unloved, and this translates into "I am unlovable." The tragic result is often isolation and loneliness. Some of these people do get married or attempt to have close relationships but still keep distance in an unconscious effort to stay safe as well as protect others from what they may perceive as their own toxicity.

> "It is those of us who have been broken that become experts at mending."
>
> — Dr. Steve Maraboli

In PTSD, as we have said, feelings of estrangement or detachment from others are considered a diagnostic symptom. What if physicians and therapists have been able to treat your glitchy and horrific memory-related problems with techniques such as EMDR...but they haven't helped you truly embrace the pain, search for meaning, and develop a new self-identity, all the while being supported and accepted by others? In this scenario, I believe that we're setting you up for ongoing difficulties with trust and intimacy...and carried grief.

Depression and negative outlook
In my experience, grief-carriers often show up in the counselor's office with what I call loss of their divine spark—that which gives purpose and meaning to our living. When their spirits remain muted, there is an ongoing hampering of the capacity to live life

with meaning and purpose. The result is often depression and a negative, cynical view of life.

Depression symptoms include sadness, inactivity, difficulty with thinking and concentrating, a significant increase or decrease in appetite, sleep disturbance, feelings of hopelessness and dejection, and sometimes suicidal thoughts or actions. While there are multiple causes of depression, my experience suggests that carried grief is a contributor for many people.

Depression sometimes masks itself as a general negative outlook on life. While some grief-carriers don't experience deep, dark depression, they suffer from a chronic, low-grade depression called "dysthymia." The world begins to look gray. They lose their full range of emotional functioning, defending against ever being really happy or really sad. Sometimes they rationalize this mood state as "just what life is like."

Similarly, feelings of meaninglessness often pervade the lives of grief-carriers. People who grieve but don't mourn often feel isolated emotionally and lack a sense of meaning and purpose. They experience a sense of soullessness, or a loss of vitality and enthusiasm for life and living. They feel empty and alone.

Negativity is another diagnostic symptom of PTSD. Can we "fix it" with antidepressants or short-term cognitive behavioral therapy, for example? I don't think so. While antidepressants and CBT are sometimes both extremely effective components of treatment, any therapy that sees traumatic grief as a short-term problem or that attempts to get rid of a symptom without also exploring the causes of that symptom is setting you up for ongoing problems.

Anxiety and panic attacks

Some grief-carriers struggle with persistent and generalized anxiety. Anxiety is often reflected in motor tension (fatigue, muscle aches, easy startle response); autonomic hyperactivity (dry mouth, gastrointestinal distress, heart racing); apprehensive expectations (fears of injury or death); and hyper-vigilance and scanning (hyper-alertness, irritability, and problems with sleep disturbance).

> "Our anxiety does not empty tomorrow of its sorrows, but only empties today of its strengths."
>
> — Charles H. Spurgeon

Again, just as with depression, there can be multiple causes of anxiety; however, I am certain that carried grief is a contributor for many people.

Anxiety sometimes shows up in the form of panic attacks. Panic is a sudden, overpowering fright. On occasion, these attacks may last for hours, though attacks are typically for a period of minutes, during which the person literally experiences terror. Panic attacks are often recurrent and episodic, though for some people they become chronic.

I have seen numerous people in counseling whose panic attacks were the doorway to get them to recognize their carried grief and learn to authentically mourn. I believe that the fear and anxiety symptoms of PTSD, which tend to be the attention-getters, are surface-level evidence of a deeper psychic injury. What traumatized grievers really need is help mourning deeply and fully—maybe even before trying to treat away their fear. I think that if traumatized grievers were first helped to understand and work on the six needs of mourning, the fear-based symptoms might naturally subside of their own accord.

Psychic numbing and disconnection

While shock and numbness are normal responses in the face of loss, some grief-carriers get so detached that they literally feel disconnected from the world around them. The result is that the world and the people in it seem unreal. Grief carriers may live their days in a daze, going through the motions yet not feeling present to others and even themselves. Some people describe this as a dream-like state with feelings of unreality. They are existing but not really alive to what is going on around them. Short-term memory loss and confusion are often also a part of this experience.

Numbing results in a feeling of existing but not really living. The muting power of numbness prevents them from experiencing or sharing in even the positive things that may be going on around them.

While numbing symptoms (apart from avoidance) have been removed from the current DSM-approved presentation of PTSD, anyone who has worked with people with PTSD will tell you that they often appear or self-describe as numb. They may also dissociate in an attempt to compartmentalize their injured selves from their still-functioning-but-flat selves.

If you have ongoing feelings of numbness and disconnection, do not despair. This simply means that, as with the other symptoms of carried grief, you have mourning work to do.

Irritability and agitation

Some grief-carriers express their pain indirectly through irritability and agitation.

These symptoms may show up at work, at home, or anywhere. It is like they are in a pressure cooker, and they are trying to release the pressure. In its extreme form, this symptom may show up as uncontrolled anger or rage.

These emotions of protest are often an unconscious attempt to fight off the underlying, more primary emotions of pain, helplessness, hurt, isolation, and aloneness. People around those exhibiting these emotions sense or experience their irritability and agitation and often begin to avoid them, resulting in more carried pain and less authentic mourning.

> "When another person makes you suffer, it is because he suffers deeply within himself, and his suffering is spilling over. He does not need punishment; he needs help. That's the message he is sending."
>
> — Thich Nhat Hanh

Irritability and aggressive, self-destructive, and reckless behavior are expressly part of the DSM-5 PTSD picture. These symptoms could be treated with antidepressants, which might help a person with PTSD feel less irritable. Similarly, Ativan or other medications might calm aggression. But would either of these treatments actually help this person understand, explore, and express the source of his emotions? No.

Substance abuse, addictions, and eating disorders
Many grief-carriers will self-treat their pain through substance abuse, addictive behaviors, or eating disorders. Modern society provides an increasing number of substances that might be abused. People are usually abusive of or addicted to a specific substance, such as alcohol, cocaine, or food. However, grief-carriers can also be addicted to activities, such as destructive relationships, sex, smoking, gambling, gaming, porn, work, exercise, achievement, over-caretaking of others, religiosity, and materialism. These substances and activities are ways the person tries to distract himself from, deny, or dampen the pain of life losses.

According to the National Center for PTSD, more than twenty percent of veterans with PTSD are also substance abusers. Six of every 10 vets with PTSD smoke.

And one in three vets who seeks treatment for substance abuse also has PTSD.

The good news is that the ready availability of these statistics means that the link between PTSD and substance abuse is widely recognized. The potentially bad news is that once the substance abuse is under control, the person may be considered "cured." While ongoing sobriety for people with PTSD who had been using is of course a step in the right direction, it does not equate to "resolution" or, more importantly, reconciliation.

Physical problems, real or imagined
One thing I know about grief is that if we don't mourn one way, it comes out another.

Many grief-carriers store the pain in their bodies. The result is that the immune system breaks down and illness surfaces. Many formal studies have documented significant increases in illness following the experience of a variety of losses in life, particularly death loss.

When we authentically mourn, these physical symptoms are normal and temporary. However, when people shut down, deny, or inhibit mourning, they sometimes assume a "sick role" in an effort to legitimize not feeling well to those around them. They "somaticize"—which means to convert into physical symptoms—their feelings of grief.

Sometimes the physical symptoms are very real; other times they are imagined. These imagined symptoms are often a silent voice crying out for the need to give expression to the carried pain. The imagined illnesses usually express themselves through multiple, vague complaints. Typically, a medical doctor can't find anything objectively wrong with the person's body.

The somaticizer may become so completely preoccupied with aches and pains and sickness that she has little or no energy to relate to others and to do the work of mourning. Even in the absence of real illness and emotional support from medical caregivers, no amount of reassurance or logic convinces her that she is not physically sick. The unconscious need to protect herself requires that this person desperately needs the belief in illness to mask feelings connected to the loss and grief.

In addition to the fight-or-flight fear-response symptoms of shortness of breath, sweating, etc., physical symptoms such as chronic pain, headaches, stomach pain, dizziness, tightness in the chest, muscle cramps, and low back pain are often seen in PTSD. In fact, veterans who have been diagnosed with psychiatric conditions are significantly more likely than others to have risk factors for cardiovascular disease, like hypertension and diabetes.

While physical symptoms are not called out in the DSM-5 criteria for PTSD, they are commonly present. And like the other symptoms in this carried-grief discussion, they can be thought of as—in the absence of physical findings during a comprehensive medical exam—indicators that something is wrong emotionally and spiritually.

For people who have experienced a traumatic event, this "something" is often unmourned grief.

Catch-up mourning for traumatic grief

In grief, the healing process is a continuum. It begins with your awareness that you are carrying unmourned grief, and it evolves to experiencing a meaning-filled life. And in between is the focus of this section: the healing process.

Healing carried grief does not happen by itself. Just as it does with present-day grief, healing old griefs requires you to identify, befriend, and actively mourn your carried pain. As I have said, time alone has nothing to do with healing. Healing requires active engagement. And even then, life losses are never "fixed" or "resolved"; they can only be soothed and integrated through actively experiencing and expressing the mixture of thoughts and feelings that arise.

> "...until you heal the wounds of your past, you will continue to bleed. You must find strength to open the wounds, stick your hands inside, pull out the core of the pain that is holding you in your past, the memories, and make peace with them."
>
> — Iyanla Vanzant

Grief is like a spiral. Spirals are unending. You can go through the same circuit again and again, but traveling up the spiral, you pass through the same symptoms at a different level, experiencing a slightly different perspective each time. They do not form discrete, static shapes because spirals can always grow and change.

The gradual movement toward transformation invites emotional, spiritual, and interpersonal growth. With the support of a compassionate companion counselor, the person's capacity to reveal her losses and make deep and lasting changes becomes possible.

In thinking about carried grief and its cumulative effects, it's helpful to consider the various significant life losses we all encounter along the way. You see, unmourned grief from your traumatic experience may not be the only cause of your ongoing symptoms. Unmourned grief often accumulates throughout life, as a result of the many common losses listed on pages 114 and 115. And if you are suffering from debilitating PTSD, especially if your symptoms seem to be disproportionately more severe than the traumatic event that unleashed them, it could be that your traumatic grief has been amplified by older, carried griefs.

> "The worst wounds, the deadliest of them, aren't the ones people see on the outside. They're the ones that make us bleed internally."
>
> — Sherrilyn Kenyon

I have had the honor of working with hundreds of people who have allowed me to support them in mourning life losses that originate from carried pain. I use the term "catch-up mourning" to describe the process that helps them experience a more considered, conscious life, rather than just drifting in a fog or living out their carried pain.

A model I have created to help in the catch-up mourning process is outlined on page 112. The entire premise of helping my fellow human beings do catch-up mourning is my belief that when we learn to be with the pain that we have up until that point denied, we retrieve those parts of ourselves that were left behind. The result is that we are able to accept and integrate those parts of ourselves. We discover that in giving voice to our mourning lies the wisdom we need to live a meaningful, purposeful life. If we mourn our carried pain, we can truly and fully live until we die.

In the broadest sense, deciding to recognize and encounter carried pain is a choice between opposites: a life devoid of deep feeling or a deeply felt life; escapist activities or meaningful activities. It means choosing between experiencing a life with its very real pains and pleasures or living in an anesthetized fog in which authentic feelings are inhibited; between a consciousness of our deepest feelings, or a vague, muted self-awareness.

Giving attention to carried pain is, in many ways, choosing between living life from a place of truth or living a lie. When you are living a lie, you are misrepresenting the reality of your experience or the truth of your being. You are allowing a disconnect between the self that resides deep within you—your true self—and the self you manifest in the world around you. For example, you are living a lie when you say you are angry but the truth is you are afraid. When you laugh but what you really feel like doing is crying. When you present yourself as having values you do not feel or hold. When you pretend a love you do not feel. When you are kind to everyone except the people you claim to love. When you profess beliefs only to win acceptance.

When you end up living a lie, you are always your own first victim because the fraud is ultimately directed at yourself. If you are living a series of lies, you do so because you feel or believe that who you really are is not acceptable. You value a delusion in someone else's mind above your own knowledge of the truth. The result is living an incongruent life and experiencing the carried grief symptoms outlined on pages 100 through 107.

As I've said, our mourning-avoidant culture invites people to carry pain and encourages them to live an inauthentic life. People are often influenced in ways that make an appreciation of authentically mourning life losses all but impossible. We learn early in life to deny feelings of loss and to wear a mask, and eventually we lose contact with our inner selves. We become unconscious to much of our inner selves in adjusting to the world around us.

Significant adults in our childhoods often encouraged us to disown fear, grief, anger, and pain because such feelings made them uncomfortable. Adults who carry grief tend to raise children who carry grief, not only through direct communication, but through their own behavior, which models for the child what is appropriate, proper, and acceptable.

The paradox is that in order to live in this environment, we often learn to "play dead" as a way of making life more tolerable. Playing dead is so common for many grief-carriers that it becomes our perception of normal. It is the familiar, the comfortable, whereas living "alive" can feel strange, even disorienting. Sadly, playing dead is a recipe for self-rejection and self-estrangement.

> "I want to feel all there is to feel, he thought. I mustn't forget I'm alive. I know I'm alive. I mustn't forget it tonight or tomorrow or the day after that."
>
> — Ray Bradbury

Those who live in the shadow of the ghosts of grief are among the many that I call the "living dead."

When we honor the presence of our current and carried grief, when we understand the need to surrender to the appropriateness of mourning our losses, we are committing to facing the pain. We are committing ourselves to look our anguish in the face and experience it in ways that allow us to begin to breathe life into our souls again.

In this book, I hope you find encouragement to gently befriend your carried grief. Instead of pulling down the blinds and shutting out light and love, you will begin the process of stepping out into the light. Slowly you will return to life—or experience it deeply for the first time—and begin living and loving in ways that put stars back into your skies.

A model for catch-up mourning

Because of our culture's grief avoidance and our medical establishment's grief pathologizing, most of us, I believe, carry grief to some extent. So, the model I describe below will help people who have virtually any psychic injury or mental health problem because carried grief is likely a contributor to your struggles. However, people with PTSD are particularly susceptible to carried grief because PTSD is not yet formally recognized as a symptom of significant loss and therefore a grief response.

I'll say it once again: grief requires mourning. And traumatic grief requires mourning that is as wide and as deep as the injury that created it. Many people with PTSD receive brief and shallow/"targeted" support when what they really need and deserve is open-ended, compassionate companionship that follows them wherever they lead.

Until you feel a renewed sense of wholeness, hopefulness, meaning, and joy in life (see signs of reconciliation on page 147), you probably need to continue to actively work on catch-up mourning.

Step 1: Acknowledge carried grief

Catch-up mourning begins with uncovering and sharing your cumulative stories of loss and pain. Before you can go forward, you must first go backward to mine your life history for unmourned losses.

As you were reading over the common symptoms of carried grief, did you recognize parts of your own symptoms picture anywhere in them? I'd like you to consider the possible sources of your carried pain. As you work to make a commitment to have the courage to proclaim your right to heal, get the help you need, and integrate the pain into your life, you may find it helpful to review the following Carried Grief Self-Inventory.

Again, the purpose of inventorying your losses and acknowledging these potential symptoms is not to discourage or shame you, but to ultimately empower you. This self-inventory is a way for you to begin to recognize and acknowledge your experience. Yes, this process can be frightening. After all, while committing yourself to healing ultimately brings a better life, it also threatens to forever alter life as you have known it. You may find that one part of you wants to heal while another resists change. Obviously, my hope is that you will have the courage to "do your work" and discover a new, more meaning-filled life.

> "One heals suffering only by experiencing it to the full."
> — Marcel Proust

Self-awareness and acknowledgment is the first step in deciding to face your carried grief and to change your life. Even if your life path has been shaped by carried grief, you are deciding you no longer need to be defined by it. You are choosing to be an active participant in your healing.

The following Loss Inventory lists many types of losses commonly suffered by humankind. I invite you to skim the list and circle or put a checkmark next to the types of losses that you have experienced. This list is not comprehensive, of course, so I'd also like you to use the blank lines that follow to write down all the significant losses in your life, including those that may not be listed here.

CARRIED GRIEF SELF-INVENTORY

COMMON LIFE LOSSES

☐ *Loss of people you love*

○ Separation (physical and/or emotional)

○ Rejection

○ Hostility/grudges

○ Illness (such as Alzheimer's, debilitating conditions)

○ Divorce

○ Abandonment/betrayal

○ Miscarriage or stillbirth

○ Death

○ Empty nest

☐ *Loss of pets*

☐ *Loss of aspects of self*

○ Self-esteem (often through physical, sexual, or emotional abuse or rape, humiliation, rejection, failure at something, or neglect)

○ Health, physical, or mental ability

○ Job (downsizing, firing, failed business, retirement)

○ Control (such as through addiction, victimization)

○ Innocence (such as through abuse, exposure to immoral behavior)

○ Sexual identity/ability/desire

○ Security (such as through crime, financial problems, war)

○ Expectations about how our lives should/would be

○ Reputation

○ Beliefs (religious, spiritual, belief in others we trusted)

○ Dreams (cherished hopes for the future)

☐ *Loss of physical objects*

○ Home (such as through a physical disaster, move, or transition into assisted living environments)

○ Linking objects (special items such as photos that carry emotional weight)

○ Money

○ Belongings (through theft or fire, etc.)

○ Nature/place (through a move, changing land use)

☐ *Loss through developmental transitions*

○ Toddlerhood to childhood

○ Childhood to adolescence

○ Adolescence to adulthood

○ Leaving home

○ Marriage

○ Having/not having children

○ Mid-life

○ Taking care of parents

○ Retirement

○ Old age

My personal loss inventory:

WHAT HAPPENS WHEN YOU DON'T MOURN

After you've completed your personal loss inventory, go back and circle or highlight those losses that you think may be contributing to your carried pain. How do you know which are most significant for you? As you're perusing your list, pause for a moment on each item and note which ones elicit the most emotion. Which make you feel the most sad? The most angry? The most fear? The most pain? Whether they seem significant on the surface or not, these are likely your deepest sources of carried grief. For example, having been fired from a job may, for you, have resulted in more carried pain than the death of a family member, especially if you mourned the death but never the job loss.

You might have noticed that this list of common losses does not specifically address traumatic losses. It is extremely common for people to have symptoms of carried grief even when they have never suffered a trauma. Instead, significant but untraumatic losses build up over time, and if they are not mourned in real time as they occur, they accumulate into a heavy load of carried grief. On the flip side, traumatized grievers are almost always carrying some older, accumulated grief in addition to their traumatic grief—so, even if the traumatic event was relatively recent, there is the potential need for catch-up mourning.

Now that you've inventoried the types of losses you've experienced in your life, I encourage you to answer the following questions. Circle the word that most applies to how you authentically feel.

1. Do you have difficulties with trust and intimacy?

   Never Seldom Occasionally Often Usually

2. Do you have a tendency toward depression and a negative outlook?

   Never Seldom Occasionally Often Usually

3. Do you have difficulties with anxiety and/or panic attacks?

Never Seldom Occasionally Often Usually

4. Do you have trouble with psychic numbing and disconnection?

Never Seldom Occasionally Often Usually

5. Do you have difficulties with irritability and agitation?

Never Seldom Occasionally Often Usually

6. Do you struggle with substance abuse, addictions, or eating disorders?

Never Seldom Occasionally Often Usually

7. Do you have any physical problems, real or imagined?

Never Seldom Occasionally Often Usually

8. Do you find it easier to take care of others than you do to care for yourself?

Never Seldom Occasionally Often Usually

9. Do you find it difficult to express your feelings?

Never Seldom Occasionally Often Usually

10. Do you find it difficult to ask for what you want from other people?

Never Seldom Occasionally Often Usually

11. Do you feel a lack of meaning and purpose in your life?

Never Seldom Occasionally Often Usually

If you identified losses in your loss inventory that still cause you twinges of pain when you think about them, and if you answered "Occasionally," "Often," or "Usually" to any of the questions above, you may be carrying grief.

Step 2: Overcome resistance to do the work

Naturally, approaching feelings that have been long been inhibited, denied, or "stuffed" can be a difficult experience. When you first begin to feel some intense emotions surrounding your carried grief, you may fear that your pain will be limitless. Many people I have helped over the years have told me some variation on "If I let myself start to feel, I may never stop." However, opening the door to carried pain, while often frightening, is necessary in the healing process.

Obviously, to begin to admit to having such frightening and powerful thoughts and feelings undermines any denial that one is "just fine." And remember, many people around you, and society in general, would *prefer* it if you were "just fine."

Sometimes when people start to do catch-up mourning, some people in their lives will label them as having problems or becoming emotionally unstable. In fact, what you are actually doing is openly acknowledging the presence of something important that deserves your attention. Each step in this process requires your courage to refuse to give in to your fears. Still, you may be tempted to take the path of least resistance, to return to your defenses and ignore the feelings within that are inviting you to acknowledge and honor them.

Yes, honor them. Honoring literally means "recognizing the value of and respecting." To honor your emotional and spiritual selves is not self-destructive or harmful; it is self-sustaining and life giving.

You must set your intention to mourn your carried grief. Having intention is defined as being conscious of what you want to experience. When you set your intention to heal unhealed wounds, you make a true commitment to positively influence the work that must be done. Essentially, you choose between living an unlived life—one that may well be made even more challenging by any stuck fear-based PTSD symptoms—and becoming an active participant in your catch-up mourning.

> "You need to be content with small steps. That's all life is. Small steps that you take every day so when you look back down the road, it all adds up and you know you covered some distance."
>
> — Katie Kacvinsky

Your decision to heal is a moment-by-moment, day-by-day choice. You take one small step forward, you commit to one particular action, and then you take the next step. By saying yes in the moment, you gradually create momentum toward your healing: "Yes, I will share one untold part of my story today."

Grievers who are able to see themselves as the center of their own healing process and are able to make choices that will serve them well in the long term find it easier to make the commitment to heal. Realizing that you are in control, that you will not be forced to do anything against your will, is critical to feeling safe as you do your work. Paradoxically, when you are assured that your, "No, I'm not ready" will be respected, you can experience the unfolding of being able to one day say, "Yes, I am ready."

Being in control of dosing your unmourned pain is the opposite of what happened when the traumatic event occurred. Now you can make choices. Reliving painful feelings and taking risks are part of the healing process. But your desire to make choices lets you ask yourself, "Is this the right time? Am I willing to go through this now? Do I want to open up to my carried pain, or do I want to shut down and continue to live in the shadow of the ghosts of grief?"

In my grief counseling practice, I have asked people with carried grief to commit to this step of the catch-up mourning process in writing. Here is how one person expressed the decision to mourn her carried grief:

I have decided to pay attention to my inner pain, to feel the feelings I've tried to stuff inside. I don't want to keep living the way I have been. I am going to choose the truth and free myself to discover peace in my heart. I have the strength and desire to explore my losses in more depth and mourn them so that I can free myself to live with new meaning and purpose in life.

The nice thing about creating a written statement such as this one is that you can then refer back to this statement as you do your work of mourning. Whenever you need motivation, you can re-read your commitment and continue with your journey toward healing.

Step 3: Actively mourn the carried grief

Actively mourning carried grief is the most painful step toward reconciling carried grief, but it is also the most liberating. On the one hand, embracing carried pain from a traumatic event as well as cumulative life losses naturally brings sorrow. On the other hand, I have seen that the discovery that it is never too late to mourn creates the energy to actually do the work necessary to heal and create a meaning-filled life.

Our feelings are the way in which we perceive our existence. They are a vital link in our relationship to others, ourselves, and the world around us. They are how we know we are alive. That is why when we shut our feelings down, we risk being among the living dead. When we disconnect ourselves from our true feelings, we have no true awareness of life. But when we stop to identify and experience our feelings, both current and long buried, we wake up.

To actively mourn your carried grief, you need permission, validation, and the space in which to safely feel. You need *sanctuary*, which is a place of refuge from external demands. A space where you are free to disengage from the outside world. A place where your need to turn inward and suspend will not be hurried or ridiculed. An empathetic grief counselor trained in the art of companioning can provide you this permission, validation, and sanctuary.

> "The best way to make your dreams come true is to wake up."
>
> — Paul Valery

I do not pretend that openly mourning carried losses, especially traumatic losses, is done easily and efficiently. Many people have carried pain for years, and when traumatic grief is added to the scales, it can feel like they tip beyond all righting.

But because PTSD is recognized as a legitimate diagnosis and is eligible for reimbursable treatment, you may well be eligible to receive ongoing care. If you can learn to actively and fully mourn your carried grief, over time and with the support of others you will achieve the kind of deep and lasting healing of your traumatic injury that only active, thorough mourning can accomplish.

I believe deep in my soul that a blessing we all instinctively seek in mourning our life losses is not to live in the absence of pain but rather to live "alive" in a way in which our pain has meaning. The process of catch-up mourning helps us discover that meaning.

The needs of mourning in carried grief

Here I would like to briefly revisit the six central needs of mourning, because if you are carrying grief, it is these same six needs that you must actively work to meet if you are to truly and deeply heal your psychic injuries. In other words, the six needs are "how" you mourn your carried grief and begin to achieve reconciliation.

Mourning Need 1: *Acknowledge the reality of the loss(es)*

Traumatized grievers typically need some guidance and modeling in acknowledging both the many primary and secondary losses created by the traumatic event but also considering past losses in their lives that may be contributing to their PTSD symptoms. While some people can easily name their griefs, many others struggle to do so. Of course, this makes sense. Identifying carried griefs can be very difficult, particularly ones that may have been denied or "stuffed" for years.

I encourage you to see a trained, compassionate counselor to help you with this mourning need as well as the other five that follow. PTSD is challenging enough, but when you combine it with other accumulated life losses, the total grief burden is usually something people need help embracing and working through.

Spending time in the beginning uncovering all significant unmourned losses will help you become more aware of the cumulative nature of grief. On the other hand, when you find that you want to focus on a particular loss, follow your instincts. Always let your symptoms, thoughts, and feelings be your guide. As your stories unfold, there will be time for you to circle back with your counselor and consider the effects of other life losses that may not have been identified at first.

Mourning Need 2: *Feel the pain of the loss(es)*

Active, authentic mourning creates what is called *perturbation*, which is "the capacity to experience change and movement." The word *feeling* originates from the Indo-European root that literally means "to touch." So, it is embracing, or touching, their feelings that activates people's natural capacity to be affected by the experiences they encounter along life's path.

Simply put, emotions need motion. The "stuckness" of PTSD is actually a symptom that you are not fully experiencing the changes created by the loss. It can be as if you've been broadsided but have not allowed yourself to reel from the impact, examine the wound, and move down the paths that lead to healing. Instead, you may still be stuck at the moment of impact, like a paused video. If this is the case for you, you may not be experiencing the necessary movement, or perturbation. This is not a disorder but rather an indication of the need for the embracing and expression of symptoms, thoughts, and feelings.

I have noticed that each time people experience and integrate some of their carried pain, they gain confidence in their capacity to regroup after the next period of emotional and spiritual work. Slowly, and with no rewards for speed, they come to discover that their denied grief does not, as they had feared, overwhelm them. If they are supported by others, they discover that they can not only invite and allow the thinking of their thoughts and the feeling of their feelings, they can survive—and ultimately thrive.

Mourning Need 3: *Remember the losses and their aftermath*

Remembering is essential to grief work. As you work to uncover the unmourned losses that have resulted in your carried grief, you will be remembering extensively. But conjuring memories of the traumatic event itself as well as its aftermath is often, as we acknowledged on page 74, tricky. As you do your catch-up mourning, how much remembering is necessary? How much is too little? How much is too much?

While I believe that sharing your traumatic memories outside of yourself is almost always essential, and the PTSD research affirms the effectiveness of treatments that in one way or another activate memories of the traumatic event, you and your counselor must work together to determine how much memory sharing is best for you.

Mourning Need 4: *Develop a new self-identity*

As you do your work of catch-up mourning, you will consider how your self-identity has been impacted not only by the traumatic event but also by other life losses. In acknowledging some painful aspects of your changed self-identity, you can mourn and sometimes release them. For example, some people with PTSD who knowingly or unknowingly continue to see themselves as victims may go on to release their feelings of victimization and embrace more empowering concepts of self-identity.

Many catch-up grievers also discover that as they work on this need, they ultimately discover some positive aspects of their changed self-identities. They often develop a renewed confidence in themselves and a more caring, kind, and sensitive self-image.

Mourning Need 5: *Search for meaning*

The search for meaning is often the centerpiece of the catch-up mourning process. Even though there are not always answers to the most difficult meaning-of-life-and-loss questions, many grief carriers ultimately find value—and even peace—in wrestling with them. Also, the process of searching for meaning in loss is lifelong. Like grief, it does not ever truly end. But you can achieve a peace in your search that allows you to live and love fully and to step out of the shadow of the ghosts of grief and into the light.

Mourning Need 6: *Receive ongoing support from others*

Grief-carriers, especially traumatized grief carriers, need the ongoing support of others in their lives to move forward in wholeness. I encourage you to involve those you love in your struggles with reconciling your carried grief. Those closest to you deserve your honesty and you, in turn, deserve the support of your friends and family.

Opening up to significant others, children, parents, siblings, and best friends about your awakening will help all these people understand the transformation you are undergoing. It will also help these people embrace the new person you are becoming.

I also urge grief-carriers who are so inclined to seek ongoing support from a support group, a spiritual leader, or others. Traumatized grievers can also often offer support to fellow grief-carriers.

Step 4: Integrate the carried grief

When people have given attention to their carried grief in ways that it deserves and demands, they begin to experience a renewed sense of wholeness. To heal in grief literally means "to become whole." The key to integration of grief is to make connections and keep making them as you learn to continue your changed life with fullness and meaning. While you have been irrevocably shaped by your losses, you can now begin to understand that you do not have to be defined by those losses.

- You become aware of how the past interfaces with the present and how the present ebbs back into the past.
- You discover that the route to healing lies not only in the physical realm but also in the emotional and spiritual realms.
- You find that the fulfillment of a life well lived is bestowed through the translation of your past into experiences that are expressed through the oral or written word.
- You come to understand that in your pain and suffering lies the awareness of the preciousness of each day on the earth.
- You discover your truth in this present moment of time and space.

Part Five

BELIEVE IN YOUR CAPACITY TO HEAL

We've talked about PTSD as an injury caused by a traumatic event—an injury that created losses of many kinds. We've also emphasized that loss naturally and automatically results in grief—the thoughts and feelings we have inside us after a loss. And to heal, we need to express our grief outside of us. In other words, we must mourn.

Now that you've had some time to consider this view of post-traumatic stress as a kind of complicated grief, how are you feeling about it? In my experience, people with PTSD often feel liberated by this understanding. They feel a sense of relief that they are normal, not abnormal. That they are injured, not ill or disordered. That what they need is not a quick patching-up that fails to acknowledge the severity and true quality of their injuries but instead a longer-term emotional and spiritual system of support.

> "Deep in your wounds are seeds, waiting to grow beautiful flowers."
>
> — Niti Majethia

Some people with PTSD, on the other hand, can be overwhelmed by this new understanding. After all, quick fixes sound good, and the concrete language of PTSD diagnoses and treatments can seem reassuring.

But if you are reading this particular book, I trust that you are searching for a new understanding of PTSD. I would guess that the medical establishment's methods for treating away PTSD have already failed you, as they so often do. And I hope you are hopeful and inspired. The mourning process is hard work, yes, but it is work that can result in more fulfillment and deeper healing than you had dared to hope for.

Setting your intention to heal

With effort, commitment, and intention, your symptoms of traumatic grief will ease, and you will find your way to a life of love and joy. Commitment goes hand in hand with the concept of "setting your intention." Intention is defined as being aware or conscious of what you want to experience. A close cousin to "affirmation," it is using the power of positive thought to envision and produce a desired result.

> "You can't patch a wounded soul with a Band-Aid."
>
> — Michael Connelly

We often use the power of intention in our everyday lives. If you have an important presentation at work, you might focus your thoughts in the days before the meeting on speaking clearly and confidently. You might envision yourself being well received by your colleagues. You have set your intention to succeed in this presentation. By contrast, if you spend your time thinking about the many ways your presentation could fail and you succumb to your anxiety, you are much less likely to give a good presentation.

How can you use this concept in your journey through traumatic grief? By setting your intention to heal.

When you set your intention to heal, you make a true

commitment to positively influence the course of your journey. You choose between being what I call a "passive witness" or an "active participant" in your grief. To heal, you must be willing to learn about the mystery of the grief journey. It can't be fixed or "resolved"; it can only be soothed and reconciled through actively experiencing the multitude of thoughts and feelings involved.

The concept of intention setting presupposes that your outer reality is a direct reflection of your inner thoughts and beliefs. If you can change or mold some of your thoughts and beliefs, then you can influence your reality. And in journaling and speaking (and praying!) your intentions, you help "set" them.

In part, you can choose whether you intend to experience spiritual pessimism or spiritual optimism. For example, if you believe that God is vengeful and punishes us for our sins by causing terrible things to happen to us, it will be next to impossible for you to make it through difficult times. Not only will you carry the pain of the loss, you will carry the guilt and blame about how sinful you are to deserve this in your life.

By contrast, if you "set your intention" to be what I would call "spiritually optimistic" and believe that embracing the pain of your losses can lead to reconciliation, you can and will survive.

"Man often becomes what he believes himself to be. If I keep on saying to myself that I cannot do a certain thing, it is possible that I may end by really becoming incapable of doing it. On the contrary, if I have the belief that I can do it, I shall surely acquire the capacity to do it even if I may not have it at the beginning."
— Mahatma Gandhi

You might tell yourself, "I can and will reach out for support in my traumatic grief. I will become filled with hope that I can and will survive this loss." Together with these words, you might form mental pictures of hugging and talking to your friends and seeing your happier self in the future.

Setting your intention to heal is not only a way of surviving the aftermath of the traumatic event (although it is indeed that!); it is a way of guiding your grief to the best possible outcome. Of course, you will still have to honor and embrace your pain during this time. By honoring the presence of your pain, by understanding the appropriateness of your pain, you are committing to facing the pain. You are committing yourself to paying attention to your anguish in ways that allow you to begin to breathe life into your soul again. That, my friend, is a very good reason to give attention to your intention. The alternative would be to shut down in an effort to avoid and deny your pain, which is to die while you are still alive.

No reward for speed

Reconciling grief does not happen quickly or efficiently. Reconciling traumatic grief, especially, takes time and hard work. In fact, "grief work" may be some of the hardest work you ever do. Because mourning *is* work. It calls on your physical, cognitive, emotional, social, and spiritual energies.

Consequently, you must be patient with yourself. When you come to trust that the pain will not last forever, it becomes tolerable. Deceiving yourself into thinking that the pain does not even exist or that you can avoid, repress, or deny it only makes it intolerable. Spiritual maturity in your grief work is attained when you embrace a paradox—to live at once in the state of both encounter and surrender, to both "work at" and "surrender to" your grief.

As you come to know this paradox, you will slowly discover the soothing of your soul. Resist the need to try to figure everything out with your head and let the paradox embrace you. You will find yourself wrapped up in a gentle peace—the peace of living at once in both *encounter* (your "grief work") and *surrender* (embracing the mystery of not "understanding").

Caring for yourself as you heal

I remind you that the word "bereaved" means "to be torn apart" and "to have special needs." Perhaps your most important special need right now is to be compassionate with yourself. In fact, the word "compassion" means "with passion." Caring for and about yourself with passion is self-compassion.

Over many years of walking with people in grief, I have discovered that most of us are hard on ourselves when we are in mourning. We judge ourselves and we shame ourselves and we take care of ourselves last. But good self-care is not only essential to your survival: it is absolutely necessary if you are to transcend your traumatic grief. To practice good self-care doesn't mean you are feeling sorry for yourself or being self-indulgent; rather, it means you are creating conditions that allow you to embrace and eventually heal the pain of your grief.

I believe that in nurturing ourselves, in allowing ourselves the time and loving attention we need to journey safely and deeply through grief, we find meaning in our continued living. We have all heard the words, "Blessed are those who mourn, for they shall be comforted." To this I might add, "Blessed are those who learn self-compassion during times of grief, for they shall go on to discover continued meaning in life, living, and loving."

When we are torn apart, one of our most important special needs is to nurture ourselves in five important realms: physical, cognitive, emotional, social, and spiritual. Following is a brief introduction to each followed by five essential self-care tasks.

The physical realm

If you are experiencing traumatic grief, your body is probably letting you know that it is distressed. Actually, one literal definition of the word "grievous" is "causing physical suffering." In fact, the neurotransmitters in your brain that are causing your fear-based symptoms are the same neurotransmitters that cause physical pain. No wonder grief and physical problems are so intertwined!

As we have said, common physical responses to loss are troubles with sleeping and low energy. You may have difficulty getting to sleep. Perhaps even more commonly, you may wake up early in the morning and have trouble getting back to sleep. During your grief journey, your body needs more rest than usual. You may also find yourself getting tired more quickly—sometimes even at the start of the day.

Muscle aches and pains, shortness of breath, feelings of emptiness in your stomach, tightness in your throat or chest, digestive problems, sensitivity to noise, heart palpitations, queasiness, nausea, headaches, increased allergic reactions, changes in appetite, weight loss or gain, agitation, and generalized tension—these are all ways your body may react to your traumatic losses. If you have a chronic existing health problem, it may get worse. The stress of grief can suppress your immune system and make you more susceptible to physical problems.

Did you notice that all of the physical symptoms of uncomplicated grief in the last paragraph can also be symptoms of PTSD? Once again, it is difficult—maybe impossible—to tease apart which physical problems are due to your grief and which to post-traumatic stress. The point is that it doesn't really matter. What matters is mourning your pain and, in the case of acute, debilitating fear-based symptoms such as panic attacks (or baseline physical problems that may be preventing mourning, such as insomnia), getting treatment so that you *can* mourn.

Good self-care is paramount at this time. Your body is the house you live in. Just as your house requires care and maintenance to protect you from the outside elements, your body requires that you honor it and treat it with respect. The quality of your life ahead depends on how you take care of your body today. Try to eat nutritious foods, get regular but gentle exercise, and allow yourself to sleep when you are tired. Also try to get some sunshine each day. Many people find that low natural light levels, especially in winter, aggravate or cause depression. If you don't live where it's sunny, try a light therapy lamp.

> "When we give ourselves compassion, we are opening our hearts in a way that can transform our lives."
>
> — Kristin Neff

Yes, I understand that when you are struggling with traumatic grief it's especially hard to muster the self-discipline and energy to take good care of yourself. So please, get others to help you. Schedule sessions with a personal trainer or ask a friend or neighbor to go for a walk with you every night. Buy or check out from the library audiobooks that will motivate you to walk while you listen. Splurge a little on healthy prepared foods in the deli section of a natural grocery store, or when friends ask what they can do to help, tell them you know you would benefit from better nutrition and you would welcome help with meals. Sometimes just a few small changes in physical care routines, and maybe spending a little more money where it matters, can make all the difference in preparing yourself physically to ease out of your worst symptoms.

Now is also a good time for a general check-up. Tell your healthcare provider about all of your symptoms. If she believes that any of your physical problems need treatment, she will address them. If you are not sleeping, for example, it may be impossible for you to find the energy to mourn. The "lethargy of grief" you are probably experiencing is a natural mechanism intended to slow you down and encourage you to care for your body, but until you are sleeping, little else will be possible. Antidepressants can sometimes ease physical symptoms as well.

Finally, be certain to "talk out" your traumatic grief. Many grieving people have taught me that if they avoid or repress talking about what happened, their bodies will begin to express their grief for them. In addition to taking good physical care of your body, you might find that the very best thing you can do for your body right now is to care for your soul—by mourning openly and honestly.

Five physical musts
Are you doing these five things to prepare yourself physically to heal your traumatic grief?

☐ I've had a complete physical within the past year or since the traumatic event (whichever is more recent).

☐ I walk or exercise at least 20 minutes a day, most days.

☐ I drink eight glasses of water every day.

☐ I eat five or more servings of fruits and vegetables each day.

☐ I am attempting to reestablish my normal sleep patterns. I lay my body down three to four times a day for 30 minutes each time to ensure that I am getting rest. If I am struggling with insomnia or sleeping too much, I will see my primary care physician to help with this issue.

The cognitive realm

Your mind is the intellectual ability to think, absorb information, remember, make decisions, and reason logically. Because traumatic events have such a profound effect on brain physiology and biochemistry, you have special needs in the cognitive realm of your grief experience. Just as your body and emotions let you know you have experienced being "torn apart," your mind has also, in effect, been torn apart.

Thinking normally after a traumatic event would be very unlikely. You are probably struggling with memory problems and may have trouble making even simple decisions. You may even feel like you are "going crazy." Essentially, your mind is in a state of disorientation and confusion. Problem-solving and higher thinking skills suffer, which can make you feel incapable of creating a plan to ease your traumatic grief.

Talk therapy, EMDR and other adjunct therapies, and, if needed, antidepressants or anti-anxiety medication can help lessen or improve over time the cognitive symptoms of traumatic grief.

Now is also a good time to use administrative technologies, if you don't already. Setting reminders on your phone, for example, can help keep you on track with lots of necessary tasks. And learning centering practices, such as breathing exercises and meditation, can be a good way for you to clear your mind when you need to and proceed with the task at hand.

You also have the power of consciously revising your distorted thoughts. Earlier in this chapter I discussed the importance of "setting your intention" to mourn and heal. Your cognitive powers are quite remarkable. Willing yourself to think something can in fact help make that something come to be. Think about your desired reality and you will be moving toward making it happen.

Five cognitive musts

Are you doing these five things to prepare yourself cognitively to heal your grief and depression?

- [ ] I talk to others about my thoughts, especially those that might be obsessive or distorted, to help me distinguish clean pain from dirty pain.

- [ ] I write things down or set reminders on my phone to help me remember essential tasks.

- [ ] I use breathing exercises or meditation to help me focus.

- [ ] I have lightened my daily schedule by eliminating tasks and obligations that are not absolutely necessary right now.

- [ ] I am postponing major life decisions until I am able to think more clearly.

The emotional realm

In Part One we explored a multitude of emotions that are often part of uncomplicated grief. These emotions reflect that you have special needs that require support from both outside yourself and inside yourself.

Befriending these emotions and practicing the self-care suggestions in this chapter can and will help you authentically mourn and heal in small doses over time. The important thing to remember is that we honor our emotions when we give attention to them.

Often traumatized mourners need something to look forward to, a reason to get out of bed each morning. It's hard to look forward to each day when you know you will be experiencing pain and sadness. Yet it is important for you to try. Even if it feels like you are only going through the motions at first, over time as you express your grief and perhaps receive help from a support group or skilled grief companion, the deliberate and daily practice of engaging in something pleasurable will help you begin to find and feel pleasure again. Reading, baking, going for a walk, having lunch with a friend, gardening, playing computer games—do whatever brings you enjoyment.

> "Acknowledging the good that you already have in your life is the foundation for all abundance."
>
> — Eckhart Tolle

Exercise is also a mood-lifter. When you move your body, your brain releases "happy" chemicals such as endorphins, dopamine, and serotonin. So physical activity not only makes your body feel better, it raises your spirits.

Research has shown that helping other people is another way to counteract symptoms such as hopelessness and depression. Consider volunteering when you are ready or committing random acts of kindness, such as walking your neighbor's dog or sending an "I love you" gift to someone just because. (In fact, I dare you to set this book down right now. Rate your mood on a scale of 1 to 10, with 1 being the most distressed. Now write someone a heartfelt note of gratitude and either pop it in the mail, e-mail it, or drop it off. After you've completed this task, rate your mood again. I'll bet your mood improved, if only a little.)

Getting involved socially will also ease your traumatic grief symptoms. The challenge, of course, is that the fear-based symptoms of traumatic grief can be a vicious cycle. You feel afraid and anxious, so you stay home and isolate yourself, but the more isolated and inactive you are, the more entrenched your fear and anxiety may become, making you even more isolated and inactive. I understand this. But I've also said that reaching out to others for help (and accepting their help) is one of the six essential needs of mourning. So find ways to connect and let others in. You *must* if you are to live and love fully again.

Five emotional musts

Are you doing these five things to prepare yourself emotionally to heal your grief and depression?

☐ I share my emotions outside of myself in various ways. I am actively mourning.

☐ I pay attention to which activities lift my spirits, and I am making an effort to do more of those activities.

☐ I schedule at least one activity each day that I enjoy.

☐ I do not judge my emotions but instead accept and honor all of them.

☐ I am talking to others about my feelings.

The social realm

The traumatic event you experienced may have resulted in a very real disconnection from the world around you. After all, you live within a circle in which a Bad Thing happened. Others live outside that circle. They may feel different or apart from you. But when you reach out to your family and friends, you are beginning to reconnect.

By being aware of the larger picture, one that includes all the people in your life, you gain some perspective. You recognize you are part of a greater whole—and that recognition can empower you. You open up your heart to love again when you reach out to others. Your link to family, friends, and community is vital to your sense of well-being and belonging.

If you don't nurture the warm, loving relationships that still exist in your life, you will probably continue to feel disconnected and isolated. You may even withdraw into your own small world and grieve but not mourn. Isolation can then become the barrier that keeps your grief from softening over time. You will begin to die while you are still alive.

Allow your friends and family to nurture you. Let them in, and rejoice in the connection. Of course, you will likely find that your friendships will change during your time of traumatic grief. Traumatized grievers often tell me how surprised and hurt they feel when friends fall away after the event. "I found out who my friends really are," they say.

Know that just as *you* are doing your best right now, your friends are doing the best they can too. They surely still care about you, but they often don't know how to be present to you in your pain. They don't know if or how to talk to you about the horrific event. Grief is awkward. They may not even be conscious of this reaction, but nonetheless, it affects their ability to support you.

The best way for you to respond in the face of faltering friendships or family relationships is to be proactive and honest. Even though you're the one who's been traumatized, you may need to be the one to phone them and keep in touch.

When you talk to them, be honest. Tell them how you're really and truly feeling and that you appreciate their support. If you find that certain friends can't handle your "trauma talk," stick to lighter topics with them and lean more heavily on the friends who can.

> "You can kiss your family and friends good-bye and put miles between you, but at the same time you carry them with you in your heart, your mind, your stomach, because you do not just live in a world but a world lives in you."
>
> — Frederick Buechner

Sometimes your friends and family members can also grow fatigued by your traumatic grief symptoms. That is, they get tired of trying to help someone who always seems negative, withdrawn, or angry. If the people in your life who are closest to you are expressing impatience with your traumatic grief, take that as a cue to seek social support from a support group and/or a grief counselor. They are not necessarily doing anything wrong, and neither are you. It may simply be that you need more help than they can offer right now, and that's OK.

There are others who can and will help you. You may be lucky enough to find one particular friend or family member who will stick by your side and listen to and support you. Sometimes this person is someone who has also experienced a traumatic event. Though no one else will grieve this loss just like you, there are often many others who have had similar experiences. We are rarely totally alone on the path of mourning. Even when there is no guide, there are fellow travelers.

If you connect with a "grief buddy," consider making a pact to call each other whenever one of you needs to talk. Promise to listen without judgment. Commit to spending time together. You might arrange to meet once a week for breakfast, lunch, or to go for a walk, for example.

Finally, consider reaching out to connect socially with people with similar spiritual beliefs. If you are a follower of a certain religion, now is the time to look into trauma support groups and other services at your place of worship. Non-religious spiritual groups sometimes meet at meditation or community centers. You may find that fellow spiritual seekers will not only help you explore your grief but also provide you with a much-needed social network right now.

Five social musts

Are you doing these five things to prepare yourself socially to heal your traumatic grief?

- ☐ I am being honest with others about what I am thinking and feeling.

- ☐ I am reaching out for help, and I am accepting help when it is offered to me.

- ☐ I am having grace with those friends and family members who seem unable to support me right now and turning to those who can.

- ☐ I am honoring my natural need to withdraw when I feel the need, but I am not isolating myself too much.

- ☐ I am looking into or connecting with new social groups— especially those made up of fellow travelers on this journey through traumatic grief.

The spiritual realm

When you are torn apart by traumatic grief, you may have many spiritual questions for which there are no easy answers: Is there a God? Why me? Will life ever be worth living again? That is why, if I could, I would encourage all of us when we are in the midst of profound grief to put down "Nurture my spirit" first on our daily to-do lists.

I believe that grief is first and foremost a spiritual journey, and therefore your traumatic grief thoughts and feelings are, in a way, a spiritual experience. When you are traumatized, you are often wrestling with deeply spiritual and existential questions. Your symptoms necessarily slow you down and make you turn inward to force you to give these questions the time and attention they deserve. In fact, it is precisely because medical models of PTSD caregiving tend to ignore the spiritual dimension of traumatic grief that they are so inadequate.

We tend to think of spirituality as uplifting and positive, but the truth is that spirituality can be deeply challenging and depressing. As the famous psychotherapist Carl Jung said, "Filling the conscious mind with ideal conceptions is a characteristic of Western theosophy, but not the confrontation with the shadow and the world of darkness. One does not become enlightened by imagining figures of light, but by making the darkness conscious."

Yes, the process of redefining your spirituality presents the biggest challenges but also promises the greatest rewards. Finding ways to actively engage your spirituality right now will help you mourn and heal.

> "In order to experience everyday spirituality,
> we need to remember that we are spiritual beings
> spending some time in a human body."
> — Barbara De Angelis

You can discover spiritual understanding in many ways and through many practices—prayer, worship, and meditation among them. You can nurture your spirituality in many places—nature, church, temple, mosque, monastery, retreat center, and kitchen table among them.

No one can "give" you spirituality from the outside in. Even when you gain spiritual understanding from a specific faith tradition, the understanding is yours alone, discovered through self-examination, reflection, and spiritual transformation.

If you attend a place of worship, you may want to visit it often in the coming weeks either for services or an informal time of prayer and solitude. (On the other hand, some trauma survivors find they need a time out from their former spiritual routine. Don't feel guilty or shame yourself if this is the case for you.) If you don't have a place of worship, perhaps you have a friend who seems spiritually grounded. Ask her how she learned to nurture her spirituality. Sometimes, someone else's ideas and practices provide just what you need to stimulate your own spiritual self-care.

Consider starting each new day with meditation or prayer. When you wake up, stretch before getting out of bed. Feel the blood coursing through your body. Listen to the hum of your consciousness. Repeat a simple phrase or prayer to yourself, such as: "Today I will live and love fully. Today I will appreciate my life." You might also offer words of gratitude: "Thank you, God, for giving me this day. Help me to appreciate it and to make it count."

I also suggest you start keeping a gratitude journal. Each night before you go to bed, recount your blessings from the day. At first you may find this challenging, but as you continue this daily practice, it will get easier and more joyful.

Think of all you have to be thankful for. This is not to deny you your overwhelming loss and the need to mourn. However, you are being self-compassionate when you consider the things that make your life worth living, too. Reflect on your possibilities for joy and love each day. Honor those possibilities and have gratitude for them.

Be grateful for your physical health and your beautiful spirit. Be grateful for your family and friends and the concern of strangers. Above all, be grateful for this very moment. When you are grateful, you prepare the way for inner peace.

For me, spirituality involves a sense of connection to all things in nature, God, and the world at large. I recognize that, for some, contemplating a spiritual life in the midst of the pain of grief can be difficult. Yet life is a miracle, and we need to remind ourselves of that, during both happy times and sad times.

When it comes to our spiritual lives, we have an abundance of choices, all of which can be doors leading to the soul. Spirituality can be found in simple things: a sunrise or sunset; the unexpected kindness of a stranger; the rustle of the wind in the trees.

If you have doubts about your capacity to connect with God and the world around you, try to approach the world with the openness of a child. Embrace the pleasure that comes from the simple sights, smells, and sounds that greet your senses. You can and will find yourself rediscovering the essentials within your soul and the spirit of the world around you.

Nurturing a spiritual life invites you to connect with nature and the people around you. Your heart opens and your life takes on renewed meaning and purpose. You are filled with compassion for other people, particularly those who have come to know traumatic grief. You become kinder, gentler, more forgiving of others as well as yourself.

Five spiritual musts
Are you doing these five things to prepare yourself spiritually to heal your traumatic grief?

    ☐ I allow myself to search for meaning and reconsider my spiritual beliefs and practices.

- [ ] I am connecting with my faith community if I find it helpful, and I am exploring other faith and spiritual communities if I am interested.
- [ ] I express my spirituality daily.
- [ ] I spend time in nature as often as I can.
- [ ] I make it a point to express gratitude in some way every day.

Reconciling your traumatic grief

Traumatized grievers have often been mired for a long time in their fear and carried grief. But as you actively mourn, you will find you can once again begin to live authentically and honestly with yourself and those around you. As your new life unfolds, you reconnect with parts of yourself that had been left behind and discover new parts of yourself that you didn't recognize before.

> "Scars are not injuries...A scar is a healing. After injury, a scar is what makes you whole."
>
> — China Miéville

You start having more fun and relaxing into the joy of being alive. Life broadens.

You have longed to be free, and now you realize you are. You have accepted responsibility for your healing and actively worked to make it so.

In grief, unlike in the medical world, healing is a holistic concept that embraces the physical, cognitive, emotional, social, and spiritual realms. Note that healing is not the same as curing, which is a medical term that means "remedying" or "correcting." You cannot remedy carried grief, but you can reconcile it. You cannot undo old injuries, but you can heal them.

Reconciliation is a term I find more appropriate for what occurs as people do the work of mourning their traumatic grief. With reconciliation comes new life energy and the capacity to be optimistic about their life journeys and to engage in the activities of being fully alive.

Reconciliation allows you to relax into the world around you. Reconciliation is not about "closure" but about "opening": opening further; learning more; connecting with the depths of your life losses; and becoming more loving, kind, and compassionate people. Instead of being among the living dead, you are awake, alive, and hope-filled.

I'm reminded of a quote from a book entitled *Patience: The Art of Peaceful Living*, by Allan Lokos. (Note that *dukkha* is a Buddhist term for uncomfortable feelings such as stress, discomfort, anxiety, and grief.)

To extinguish a fire we don't throw water on the flames, we throw water on what is burning. Fire exists because a fuel (wood, paper) has been heated to a point where it becomes combustible. To put out the fire we must cool the fuel so that it can no longer burn. The same is true of extinguishing dukkha. *We cool the fuel, which, in the case of* dukkha, *is the causes and conditions that bring about suffering. In other words, we do what is necessary to change that which causes* dukkha. *Thus, we stop bringing about our unhappiness.*

Likewise, reconciling traumatic grief requires cooling not just the symptoms but also the causes and conditions that created the grief. We cannot erase the traumatic event as if it never happened, however, but we must acknowledge it as the source of the grief and our symptoms, and we embrace and express it, which is the process that cools it.

CLOSURE: A MISNOMER

Sometimes well-intentioned but misinformed people will ask you that dreaded question, "Do you have closure?" Sometimes they will phrase it differently, asking, "Have you recovered?" or "Are you over it?" or "Have you let go?"

Without doubt, you will have someone, with seeming great authority, tell you that if you haven't put your grief and mourning behind you, you aren't really trying to achieve "closure." Keep in mind what Shakespeare once observed: "Everyone can master grief but he that has it."

Webster's Dictionary defines closure as "finished, ended." Yet in my nearly forty years of companioning thousands of people in grief, and in my own personal loss experiences, I have come to realize that closure is often a projected goal of those who have never walked the walk.

Grief never ends, and you are a different person after the traumatic event than you were before the event. There is no closing, there is only journeying. So, transformation ("an entire change in form"), YES. Closure ("finished, ended"), NO!

When someone asks you if you have "closure," do remember to have grace, for they know not what they do.

The transformative nature of grief

Traumatic grief is a spiritual, transformative journey. I'm certain you have discovered that you have been changed by the trauma you experienced and the losses it created. Many mourners have said to me, "I have grown from this experience. I am a different person."

Now, don't take me the wrong way. Believe me, I understand that the growth resulted from something you would much have preferred to avoid. While I have come to believe that our greatest gifts often come from our wounds, these are not wounds we masochistically go looking for. When others offer untimely comments like, "You'll grow from this," your right to be hurt, angry, or deeply sad is taken away from you.

Yet you are changing and growing nevertheless as a result of the traumatic event you experienced. We as human beings can't help but be forever changed by profound loss. You may discover that you are developing new attitudes. You may be more patient or more sensitive to the feelings and circumstances of others, especially those suffering from trauma and loss. You may have new insights that guide the way you live your new life. You may have developed new skills or ways of viewing humankind or the world around you.

"It may be hard for an egg to turn into a bird, but it would be a jolly sight harder for it to learn to fly while remaining an egg. We are like eggs at present. And you cannot go on indefinitely just being an ordinary, decent egg. We must be hatched or go bad."

— C.S. Lewis

Your transformation probably also involves exploring your assumptions about life. Loss invites this type of exploration. Your loss experiences have a tendency to transform your values and priorities. Every loss in life calls out for a new search for meaning, including a natural struggle with spiritual concerns, often transforming your vision of your God and your faith life.

Finally, your transformation may well include a need to do and be all you can be. In some ways, traumatic loss seems to free the potential within. Questions such as "Who am I? What am I meant to do with my life?" often naturally arise during grief.

Answering them inspires a hunt. You may find yourself searching for your very soul.

Yes, sorrow is an inescapable dimension of our human experience. We love and so we grieve. We become attached and thus are torn apart. We rejoice and then we suffer. And in our suffering, we are transformed. While it hurts to suffer loss, the alternative is apathy, or the inability to suffer, and it results in a lifestyle that avoids human relationships to avoid suffering.

You have many choices in living the transformation that traumatic grief has brought to your life. You can choose to visualize your heart opening each and every day. When your heart is open, you are receptive to what life brings you, both happy and sad. By staying open and present, you create a gateway to your healing.

When this happens you will know that the long nights of suffering in the wilderness have given way to a journey toward the dawn. You will know that new life has come as you celebrate the first rays of a new light and a new beginning.

A FINAL WORD

You are not disordered. You are living in a society that is disordered, a society addicted to labels, quick fixes, and yes, happiness. To borrow a phrase from the musical group R.E.M., we "shiny, happy people" want to pretend that bad things don't happen, that life should be nothing but fun, fun, fun. And when something bad does happen, we encourage ourselves and others to "let go," "put it behind us," and "move on" as quickly as possible.

> "You were born a child of light's wonderful secret—you return to the beauty you have always been."
>
> — Aberjhani

I want happiness for you. I want meaning for you. I want joy for you. But I know that you cannot deeply and truly achieve these things without also openly acknowledging, embracing, and working through the bad things. None of us can.

There is simply no getting around the fact that human life is a complicated mixture of experiences. I am sorry that along the way you had to experience something traumatic. Many of us do. In fact, when you set aside the strict DSM criteria for what can be considered a traumatic event, I would say that almost all of us experience one or more traumatic events or situations during our lives.

I hope I have helped you understand that PTSD is a kind of a grief. Grief is normal and natural. Your traumatic grief is normal and natural, no matter how much our society's grief-phobia might have made you believe otherwise.

And how do you heal your traumatic grief? By expressing it. By mourning it fully and actively in all five domains of your self—physical, cognitive, emotional, social, and spiritual.

Yes, grief and mourning are the missing piece in the current puzzle of PTSD. I know you've felt all along that something important was missing or you wouldn't be reading this book.

Now that you've found what's been missing, you can put it into place in your life. You can begin to actively work your six needs of mourning. You can find ways to acknowledge what happened, embrace the pain, remember, reconstruct your self-identity, search for meaning, and get help from others.

I am so hopeful for your healing and your future. You see, I know that when it comes to healing grief, mourning works. I've spent the last forty years of my life learning about it, facilitating it, teaching it, witnessing it, and, of course, doing it. It is not easy because life is not easy. But it's real, it's rewarding, and ultimately, it's transforming.

I hope we meet one day. Godspeed.

Healing Your Traumatized Heart

100 Practical Ideas After Someone You Love Dies a Sudden, Violent Death

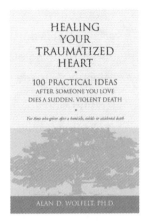

Death is never easy, but for families and friends affected by a sudden, violent death, grief is especially traumatic. Deaths caused by accidents, homicide, and suicide violate our moral, spiritual, and social codes. Things are not the same, nor will they ever be again. Persistent thoughts and feelings about what the death may have been like for the person who died—and what might have been done to prevent it—color the grief process. Strong feelings of anger and regret are also common. Understanding and expressing these feelings helps survivors, over time and with the support others, come to reconcile their loss.

Most books about trauma are written for mental health caregivers. This book is for the mourner. It offers 100 practical ideas to help them through their traumatic loss. Some of the ideas explore the basic principles of traumatic grief and mourning. The remainder give practical, proactive suggestions for moving beyond the trauma and embracing their grief.

ISBN 978-1-879651-32-6
128 pages • softcover • $11.95

Companion
PRESS

All publications can be ordered by mail from:

Companion Press
3735 Broken Bow Road
Fort Collins, CO 80526
Phone: (970) 226-6050
www.centerforloss.com

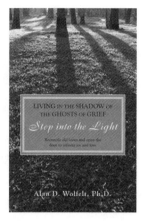

Living in the Shadow of the Ghosts of Grief

Step into the Light
Reconcile old losses and open the door to
infinite joy and love

Are you depressed? Anxious? Angry? Do you have trouble with trust and intimacy? Do you feel a lack of meaning and purpose in your life? You may well be living in the shadow of the ghosts of grief.

When you suffer a loss of any kind—whether through abuse, divorce, job loss, the death of someone loved or other transitions—you naturally grieve inside. To heal your grief, you must express it. That is, you must mourn your grief. If you don't, you will carry your grief into your future, and it will undermine your happiness for the rest of your life.

This compassionate guide will help you learn to identify and mourn your carried grief so you can go on to live the joyful, whole life you deserve.

ISBN 978-1-879651-51-7
160 pages • softcover • $13.95

Companion
PRESS

All publications can be
ordered by mail from:

Companion Press

3735 Broken Bow Road
Fort Collins, CO 80526

Phone: (970) 226-6050
Fax: 1-800-922-6051

www.centerforloss.com

The Paradoxes of Mourning
Healing Your Grief with Three Forgotten Truths

When it comes to healing after the death of someone loved, our culture has it all wrong. We're told to be strong when what we really need is to be vulnerable. We're told to think positive when what we really need is to befriend the pain. And we're told to seek closure when what we really need is to welcome our natural and necessary grief.

The paradoxes of mourning are three Truths that grieving people used to respect but in the last century seem to have forgotten. In fact, our thinking about loss has gotten so mixed up that the Truths can now seem backward, or paradoxical. Yet the paradoxes are indeed true, and only by giving yourself over to their wisdom can you find your way.

Truth One: You must say hello before you can say goodbye.

Truth Two: You must make friends with the darkness before you can enter the light.

Truth Three: You must go backward before you can go forward.

In the tradition of the Four Agreements and the Seven Habits, this compassionate and inspiring guidebook gives you the three keys that unlock the door to hope and healing.

ISBN 978-1-61722-222-1
136 pages • hardcover • $15.95

Companion
P R E S S

*All publications can be
ordered by mail from:*

Companion Press
3735 Broken Bow Road
Fort Collins, CO 80526
Phone: (970) 226-6050
www.centerforloss.com

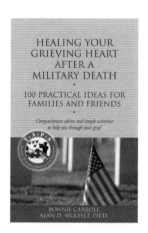

Healing Your Grieving Heart After a Military Death
100 Practical Ideas for Families and Friends

by Bonnie Carroll and Alan. D. Wolfelt

When a loved one dies during military service, the grief of survivors is unique. The military and its culture pervade so many aspects of the days and weeks following the death. And because military deaths are often sudden and violent, the traumatic nature of the loss creates a two-part grief—one focused on the manner in which the person died, the other focused on the long-term repercussions of life without this special person.

This guide acknowledges the mixture of sadness, pride, anger, and guilt that often characterizes grief after a military death, including in the event of a military suicide, and offers ideas for constructively expressing thoughts and feelings. Special mention is made of the Tragedy Assistance Program for Survivors (TAPS) and the resources it makes available to military loss survivors. Anyone whose life has been touched by a military death will find compassionate understanding and healing guidance in the pages of this handbook.

ISBN 978-1-61722-234-4
128 pages • softcover • $11.95

Companion
PRESS

All publications can be ordered by mail from:

Companion Press

3735 Broken Bow Road
Fort Collins, CO 80526

Phone: (970) 226-6050
Fax: 1-800-922-6051

www.centerforloss.com

Reframing PTSD as Traumatic Grief

How Caregivers Can Companion Traumatized Grievers Through Catch-Up Mourning

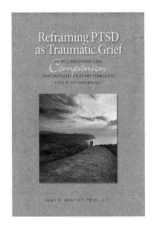

In this guide for counselors and caregivers, Dr. Wolfelt reframes PTSD as a form of grief. Helping PTSD sufferers mourn their unacknowledged and "carried" grief over the traumatic events that caused their symptoms is the key to helping them heal. Rather than seeking to quickly treat away symptoms of PTSD, caregivers who follow Dr. Wolfelt's "companioning" philosophy will instead see the natural and necessary PTSD symptoms as indicators that the sufferer needs additional support and encouragement to express himself. This holistic new approach acknowledges clinical PTSD treatments as part of the solution while emphasizing that authentic mourning is the primary and most essential healer.

ISBN 978-1-61722-213-9

144 pages • hardcover • $29.95

Companion
P R E S S

All publications can be ordered by mail from:

Companion Press
3735 Broken Bow Road
Fort Collins, CO 80526
Phone: (970) 226-6050
www.centerforloss.com

Training and
Speaking Engagements

To contact Dr. Wolfelt about speaking engagements or training
opportunities at his Center for Loss and Life Transition,
email him at DrWolfelt@centerforloss.com.